W9-BRD-733

"The author of this book is witty, wise, and happily, very practical. Using her own experience with her daughter, as well as her training as a psychologist, she guides us through the shoals of parenting and reassures us that while parenting a daughter is not smooth sailing, it is possible with a little help—and this book is quite helpful. For example, almost all parents of teenagers are going to get carved up by their child from time to time, and it's nice to know that the constant criticism is part of the teen's passage rather than one's own terminal defects. Also welcome are the many chapter tips, including the ones that help us understand obsessive behavior with phones and texting. The book is not only extremely sensible, it's terrifically readable. You get to laugh at yourself, and learn valuable information at the same time."

—Pepper Schwartz, PhD, American sociologist and sexologist,
professor at the University of Washington in Seattle, WA,
and author of *201 Questions to Ask Your Kids*

"In *Parenting a Teen Girl*, Lucie Hemmen brings expertise, common sense, and a no-drama approach to the challenge of raising girls with respect and love. Her ideas are clear, realistic, and powerful, and her steady guidance will help you bring confidence and skill to your dealings with teen girls or, for that matter, with anyone. Her teachings are so universal and wise that we could all do well to learn from them, no matter the age or gender of the people we interact with."

—Frank Andrews, PhD, professor at the University of California,
Santa Cruz and author of The Art and Practice of Loving

"*Parenting a Teen Girl* busts through many myths and helps parents stop catastrophizing and start connecting with their teen girls. Face your fears head-on and learn concrete steps to tackle common problems such as oversharing in social media and moodiness. You can learn to stop complaining about your teen girl and starting connecting to her."

—Lara Honos-Webb, PhD, author of The Gift of Adult ADD and
Listening to Depression

"This is the instruction book we always wished our children came with. Hemmen provides straight talk, practical tips, and an empathetic understanding of the challenges that teen girls and parents face today."

—Lisa M. Schab, LCSW, author of *The Anxiety Workbook for Teens* and *Beyond the Blues*

"*Parenting a Teen Girl* will help parents understand their daughters' behavior and experiences and create healthier connections with them. Through real-life examples and reflective exercises, Hemmen encourages parents to increase their self-awareness and teaches them to choose their responses rather than react to the chaos that life with a teen daughter can create."

—Sheri Van Dijk, MSW, RSW, psychotherapist and author of *Don't Let Your Emotions Run Your Life for Teens, The Bipolar Workbook for Teens,* and *Calming the Emotional Storm*

"As an Internet expert, educator of teens and parents, and mother of two girls, I appreciate Hemmen's coverage of the issues most relevant to raising teen girls in today's world. The book hits all the most important targets without lapsing into long, academically dense discourse. Readers won't get that overwhelmed and hopeless feeling regarding the state of today's teenage girls! In fact, the book energizes as it informs. I love that the book offers practical tips parents can plug in immediately—especially regarding how to guide teens in the tech world. Hemmen's compassion, understanding, and humor make the book a quick and valuable read."

—Lori Getz, Internet safety expert and founder of Cyber Education Consultants

Parenting a Teen Girl

A Crash Course on Conflict, Communication & Connection with Your Teenage Daughter

LUCIE HEMMEN, PhD

New Harbinger Publications, Inc.

Publisher's Note

This publication is designed to provide accurate and authoritative information in regard to the subject matter covered. It is sold with the understanding that the publisher is not engaged in rendering psychological, financial, legal, or other professional services. If expert assistance or counseling is needed, the services of a competent professional should be sought.

Distributed in Canada by Raincoast Books

Copyright © 2012 by Lucie Hemmen
             New Harbinger Publications, Inc.
             5674 Shattuck Avenue
             Oakland, CA 94609
             www.newharbinger.com

Cover design by Amy Shoup
Text design by Tracy Marie Carlson
Acquired by Jess O'Brien
Edited by Jean Blomquist

All Rights Reserved

FSC
www.fsc.org
MIX
Paper from
responsible sources
FSC® C011935

RAINFOREST ALLIANCE
CERTIFIED

Library of Congress Cataloging in Publication Data

Hemmen, Lucie.
  Parenting a teen girl : a crash course on conflict, communication, and connection with your teenage daughter / Lucie Hemmen.
     p. cm.
  Includes bibliographical references.
  ISBN 978-1-60882-213-3 (pbk. : alk. paper) -- ISBN 978-1-60882-214-0 (pdf e-book) -- ISBN 978-1-60882-215-7 (epub)
  1. Teenage girls. 2. Parenting. 3. Parent and child. I. Title.
  HQ798.H446 2012
  305.235'2--dc23

           2012011749

Printed in the United States of America

14   13   12

10   9   8   7   6   5   4   3   2   1

First printing

I dedicate this book to my incredible mom—
the best writing support and mother I could possibly ask for.

Thanks, Mom!

Contents

Acknowledgments

I am very grateful to my wonderful family and friends for supporting me in this adventure. Thanks, Mom and Dad, for planting the seed that I'd someday write a book and for making your home my writing office. Thanks, Jeff, for your consistent support. Thank you, Marley and Daisy, for allowing me to be so audacious as to write a book about parenting teen girls. Thank you, Cara, for being the most enthusiastic and loving sister I could ask for.

This book would not be possible without my wonderful teen clients, who have taught me so much and allowed me to pause during sessions to grab pad and pen to capture ideas they inspired. Their willingness to share themselves and their lives has been my motivation to organize and present what I've learned to share with other parents.

I love and thank my ABCs—Andrea Hultzen, Beth Wann, and Carrie Morris—for being the best friends a person could ask for and absolutely great writing support. Also, I thank my dear friends and colleagues Tom Western, Jesse Burgess, Greg Bruno, Heidi Bruce, and Tara Leonard for their convincing confidence in me and the material. I am very grateful to Jess O'Brien and New Harbinger Publications for taking me on as a new author and to Jean Blomquist for being an absolute dream editor. And I thank Joanna Doubleday for holding my hand firmly as I entered the alternate universe called social networking and Internet marketing.

1

Talking Trash about Teens:
A Reality Check

Congratulations, you have a teenage daughter! Never heard this kind of enthusiasm for parenting your teen daughter? More likely, you've been warned about the teen years since she was in diapers: "Enjoy her now; she'll be a teenager someday." Instead of feeling supported as the parent of a teen girl, you may often feel lonely, overwhelmed, and confused. You aren't always sure who can help you or if you can even seek help without feeling embarrassed, judged, or exposed.

You May Be Noticing:

○ Friends ask about your daughter with wary curiosity. It seems that people expect the worst now that she's a teenager.

○ When you mention you have a teen daughter to someone, facial expressions turn sympathetic, as if you've just disclosed a serious medical issue.

○ Fewer people seem to "get it" than in the old days, when you faced teething and pacifier addiction.

Our cultural pessimism about teen girls also impacts the way girls experience the public. Instead of feeling celebrated and acknowledged as valuable community members, teen girls often feel judged, patronized, or avoided.

Teen Girls Notice:

○ Scornful looks from adults, especially when teens are in groups

○ Eyes hastily averted, as if people are uncomfortable seeing them

○ Intrusive staring that makes them feel unwelcome, devalued, or sexualized

Why this mutual sense of wariness? Teen girls freak people out! Given to intermittent displays of sullenness, lack of conversational enthusiasm, and provocative clothing choices, girls navigating this stage of development evoke discomfort in our culture and even in our homes. If you've felt ripples of worry since your daughter's impending thirteenth birthday, you're not alone. You've been affected by the cultural fear and bad attitude toward teens that affects everybody.

When asked to reflect on his feelings about teen girls, Josh, dad of a fourteen-year-old, answered this way: "Teen girls made me uncomfortable. They seemed too brazen. Maybe I only noticed the ones who were working hard to stand out." Laura, mom of two teen daughters, said, "I was in denial. I thought they'd stay little forever. Then, *boom!* One day, every interaction becomes an argument."

Conversation Starter

Ask your daughter how she's treated in the world. Start by asking her where she feels most welcome and comfortable in the community. Which stores, food establishments, or coffee houses welcome her and other teens and treat them with respect? Where does she feel least welcome? Which businesses or establishments are unwelcoming or suspicious of teens?

Asking these questions enlightened one dad. He learned that his daughter and her friends wouldn't shop in certain stores because they felt store owners eagle-eyed them, as if they were shoplifters. Because this dad listened in an open and curious way, he learned a lot from his daughter, who happened to be in a talking mood.

Tell your daughter about your own experiences as a teenager. How were you treated by adults and establishments? How did you feel in public? If you dreaded ordering in restaurants or being out in public with your parents, share the memory with her. You can validate her feelings by saying something like this: "I understand you feel embarrassed being out in public with me sometimes. I felt that way too, when I was your age."

Even if you do a great job with this conversation starter, your daughter may not be in a mood to talk. If she passes, at least she knows you're interested in her. If she engages, you may learn something you didn't know about her experience in the world.

Major Trash Sites

For a reality check on the cultural pessimism that saturates parents and daughters alike, let's take a look at two major trash sites that create teen-girl negativity: the media and social comparison.

Trash Site #1: The Media

Good news about teens is rarely a media topic, while bad news is blown up and sensationalized. It's hard to avoid bad news about teens engaging in activities like these:

- Binge drinking

- Sexual "hookups"

- Self-mutilation

- Shoplifting

- Violence

- ○ Vandalism

- ○ Drug abuse

Salacious headlines, teen-trashing books, and titillating TV story lines do nothing to support your parenting or benefit your sanity. To capture the attention of readers, viewers, and consumers, teens are relentlessly depicted as scandalous, shallow, and troubled. Because isolated incidents can create a huge emotional impact, a media swarm gives the impression that relatively uncommon events are catastrophically epidemic. For example, attention to girl bullying has been crucial and beneficial in many ways. It's a real problem that warrants thoughtful attention. The avalanche of press, however, reduced the issue to "mean teens," which locks teen girls into a distorted stereotype and creates a belief that bad behavior among girls is normal, inevitable, and ubiquitous, which it is not.

Yes, teen girls challenge us with issues that warrant intelligent, caring attention. No, we don't benefit from the media's soulless agenda to shock and disturb us when we're already struggling to do our best. You've heard from the media. But do you really know what's going on with teens? Test your knowledge with the following exercise.

Exercise: Do You Know What's Really Going On with Teens?

True or False:

_____ Teen drug use is breaking records.

_____ Teen sex is on the rise.

_____ More teens are smoking cigarettes.

_____ Alcohol abuse is rampant.

_____ Parental influence decreases during teen years.

Ready for the surprising news? All of the above are false. American teens are not the train wrecks the media would have you believe. In fact, high school and youth trends reported by the National Institute on Drug Abuse (2010) indicate many of the above issues have significantly *decreased* in severity since we—the parents of teens—were in high school.

FOCUSING ON WHAT'S REAL

While life with teen girls is not a day at the beach, over-the-top negative buzz insidiously conditions a cultural pessimism that undermines focus on real issues and actual challenges. So what *is* true?

Bad news sells. Media headlines created for their shock value grab the attention of readers while they also pollute public opinion about teens. The media focuses on teen problems while the good news, of which there is plenty, is largely ignored.

Teens are intense. Developmentally they're experimenting with how to behave in the world. Parents never know what to expect, yet are compelled to make daily choices balancing their teen's freedom with safety. When your tenacious teen pressures you to say yes to a plan she explains with too much speed and too little detail, life is intense.

American teens are not the train wrecks the media would have you believe.

Teens are high maintenance. Teen girls consume parental energy, time, food, money, and space. They have complicated and challenging lives, and need a lot of help from parents (driving, shopping, feeding, listening, guiding, supervising, and loving). While their self-focus is developmentally appropriate, the high demand for parental support is exhausting.

Once we've set aside the negative thinking that's endemic in our culture, we can focus on the real challenges:

○ How do we keep teens safe while, at the same time, extend their freedom?

○ How do we encourage their high achievement while protecting healthy, balanced development?

- How do we encourage communication without driving them into silence?

- How do we deal with the role of technology in their lives?

- How can we feel better about ourselves as parents?

This book will address these and other challenges so you will feel confident moving through these teen years with your daughter.

Trash Site #2: Social Comparison

Talking about teen girls with your peers is a natural and often beneficial activity. At best, talking with other parents allows you to vent, feel support, and exchange helpful information. If you talk to people who are creative, compassionate, and optimistic, the social support will feel great. However, when talking for social support leads to social comparison, things start feeling bad. *Social comparison* is the process of evaluating yourself, or your daughter, in relation to others. It entails making judgments, usually based on limited information.

Social comparison can exacerbate feelings of insecurity about yourself as a parent. Or you can feel frustrated with your daughter for having a problem that makes her life (and yours) more difficult. When talking with other parents, or even when merely observing the situations they *seem to* have with their daughters, it's easy to fall into the trap of comparing and judging yourself or your daughter as "better" or "worse."

HOW SOCIAL COMPARISON AFFECTS TEEN GIRLS

Whether you make a lot of social comparisons or just a few, you can be sure that your daughter marinates in social comparisons all day long. Developmentally, it's impossible for her to avoid. Teen girls constantly compare themselves to friends, enemies, fashion models, actresses, and fictional characters. Your daughter develops a sense of who she is—and isn't—by comparing herself to others.

In fact, much of what sounds like teen girl gossiping is actually your teen analyzing others in order to see where she fits on different spectrums. When her observations about others seem consistently negative, she is actually working on feeling okay about herself. She may feel better by comparison when she amplifies the negative traits of others. Or she may feel worse when she compares herself with idealized others, such as famous people, fashion models, or a high-achieving sibling. Either way, teen girls struggle with feelings of insecurity and inadequacy.

In class, your daughter knows who performs better than her and who performs worse. She has ideas about whose hair is more beautiful and whose body is more attractive. Can you imagine how browsing through a fashion magazine or watching the latest reality show affects your daughter's assessment of herself? Her life, friends, clothes, hair, and body can't compare with the sizzling splash factor these sources portray. On the other hand, if a neighbor's daughter just got busted for shoplifting, your daughter may feel compelled to let you know how lucky you are to have her.

You can't stop your daughter's automatic habit of comparing herself to others—we all do it in one way or another—but you can make sure you don't add fuel to the fire. Even extremely well-intentioned parents make the mistake of verbalizing ways in which they compare their daughter unfavorably. You may ask her why she isn't more like her sister, her brother, the neighbor, or you. You have seen how comparing your teen to others detonates a bomb inside her. Whether she explodes at you or implodes inside herself, it's painful and harmful. It will not positively motivate improved behavior, and, more dangerously, it can provoke worrisome behavior and poor self-concept in your daughter. If you have done this a little or a lot, simply forgive yourself right now and commit to abstaining from articulating comparisons in the future.

> Your daughter develops a sense of who she is—and isn't—by comparing herself to others.

REDIRECTING THOUGHTS

Instead of engaging in social comparison, redirect your thoughts in a more positive and productive direction. When you find yourself thinking something like *Wow, the neighbor kid, Piper, is driving already. Why is my Natalie lagging at making that happen? When I was a kid, we all drove the second we were old enough. Why isn't Natalie more on top of things?* you can stop and redirect your thoughts: *Yikes! Thinking like that almost triggered me into ranting at Natalie. That would have gone nowhere fast. How can I think about this more optimistically?*

Hmmmm… Kids are under a lot of pressure to grow up fast. Maybe Natalie wants to take her time, slow things down. Maybe she enjoys the comfort of riding with me. Some of our best talks happen in the car. Or maybe she has some fears about driving. I'll make a point to ask what her driving plan is and how I can support her. Now that you've adjusted your thoughts and attitude, you are likely to have a much better approach and experience talking to your daughter.

A mom of two teenagers shares her experience with social comparison:

I come from a very competitive family, and when we get together, everyone brags about their kids. My son is a gifted athlete, so everyone is eager to hear about his latest accomplishments. My daughter's talents and qualities have always been subtler and therefore harder for some people to appreciate. While she is very funny, kind, and social, she's not interested in sports, nor is she academically high achieving. Instead of getting sucked into competitive conversations with my family members, I find ways to otherwise occupy myself, or I just sit and listen. I don't let myself get pulled into comparing my daughter to the high-performing kids. I remind myself that my job is to help my daughter connect with who she is and how she wants to grow. She's not my personal project to manage and show off.

This is one dad's story of how comparing his daughter to teammates almost resulted in his daughter quitting her sport:

My wife told me many times to keep my mouth shut after games. I couldn't seem to help telling my daughter what she could have done better and who played well compared to who messed up. I thought I was helping her be a better player. Then my daughter wanted to quit but was too afraid to tell me. My wife blamed me for this development. I took a suggestion and wrote my daughter a note letting her know that if she continued to play, I would completely back off. I promised to give her positive feedback or no feedback at all. It worked out really well, and she's still playing. My wife is much happier with me too.

Next time you catch yourself comparing, remember that there's a wide range of parents and teens out there. Your analysis will look better or worse depending on your point of reference, your mood, and so on. Since people are complicated and comparisons are made based on limited information or superficial observations, what appears enviable may not be. Alternately, parents or teens who appear to be train wrecks often have strengths and qualities we may not notice. How many times have we judged people only to find out later that our impressions were mistaken?

Getting Past Pessimism and Trash Talk

Life gets better when we commit to identifying and expanding strengths, in teen girls and in ourselves as supports. Even negative situations with teen girls have positive elements, and expanding the positive is much more productive than panicking about the negative. When we regard teens with a positive, optimistic attitude, they give us their best. When we micromanage them or convey low expectations and suspicion, they become resentful, flail, or go rogue. Our approach needs to support the outcome we want.

Have you ever observed an adult, perhaps a teacher or a coach, who seems blessed with the ability to connect with teen girls? Most of these people excel in connecting because they are genuinely positive, interested, and curious. Such individuals are generally warm, kind, supportive, and accepting. They possess goodwill and optimism, which they exude toward teen girls. Hungry for the sunlight of positive adult attention, expectation, and interaction, teen girls radiate their light for people who engage the best in them. Even though teen girls often seem disinterested, your willingness to fearlessly extend optimistic goodwill can reap significant results. The alternative is getting mired in worry and negativity.

People Are Not Problems

When people are saturated in a "problem" mentality, anxiety increases while parenting skills decrease. Even when times are hard with teen girls, it's important to resist seeing them as problems. People are not problems; problems are problems. And problems will definitely arise as you parent your teen daughter. When faced with a perceived problem, it's easy to panic and want to stomp it out like a brush fire on the living room rug. The "stomping" response may feel compelling in the moment, yet it never creates good results. More seriously, stomping injures relationships and prevents the resolution of issues.

When parents panic and become problem focused, their teen girls feel like their parents care more about the problem than about them. This seems especially true for self-regulatory issues like eating disorders and self-cutting. Teen girls want parents to see them as people first—willing to show interest, curiosity, and concern about what is going on, *even if* the teen has trouble talking about it. When teens feel the love first and concern for the problem second, they are more available to collaborate *with* the parent *against* the problem. In this way, teen girls and their parents become allies against the problem. Try on this new way of thinking and see how it feels:

Your teen girl is *not* the problem. When her behavior disappoints you, enrages you, or scares you to death, she is not the problem. Even on a really bad day, she is not the problem.

You are *not* the problem. When you observe yourself behaving horribly with your daughter, the child you planned to love and cherish always, you are not the problem. Even on your worst parenting day, you are still not the problem.

Problems, or challenges, are a guaranteed part of parenting. Fortunately they don't always mean that something is going horribly wrong. Often they are a call to pay attention and think creatively. Exercise your mind by trying to identify strengths surrounding the problem, or resources you can utilize for the solution. Also identify positive intentions in teen behaviors that are problematic. When teen girls feel your attempts to align with them and their positive intentions, they allow some level of connection instead of shutting down.

Even really inappropriate behavior contains a kernel of good intention. For example, the teen girl who comes home drunk may be experimenting with separation, risk taking, and expanding social connections. Learning to recognize and acknowledge the kernel helps you address the behavior with your daughter because she doesn't feel completely reduced (in your eyes) to whatever choice just created the problem. Even though her behavior is unacceptable, *she* is acceptable.

If you can, expect problems or challenges to appear regularly. Turn your mental dial setting to *Yes, there will be problems.* Instead

> Your teen girl
> is *not* the
> problem....
> You are *not*
> the problem.

10

of feeling shocked and betrayed by the problems, accept and expect problems to come and go. By doing this, you stand on relatively stable ground no matter what's going on. Problems are more productively handled when you expect a certain amount of turbulence and surprise behavior by your teen daughter.

Here's how smashing pessimism and trash talk allows your thinking to shift toward optimism and a solution orientation:

Pessimism	Optimism
I can't believe the way she speaks to me! How did I raise such an absolute brat?	*A lot of her behavior is developmentally appropriate. Instead of getting offended, I will respond to the behavior.*
Her flakiness and irresponsibility are a huge problem!	*She needs support with organization. How can I help her?*
Her selfishness is a huge turnoff! How did this happen?	*Teens are by nature self-focused. Part of my job is to broaden her awareness of others.*
She just wants me when she needs something.	*She relies on me to meet many of her needs. We will find a balance between dependence and independence.*

More Tips to Cultivate Optimism

Focus on optimism. Here are a few tips to help you:

Memory lane: Keep little-girl pictures of her around. Tell her a random story of her childhood or share a reflection from time to time. It's good for both of you to connect to positive feelings about the child that she was. Pull out old pictures you haven't seen for a while and post them somewhere unexpected in the house. Even if she's been a terror all week, you can still say, "I remember your Little Mermaid phase. You wore your Ariel costume everywhere. Even then, you were really creative with your clothing choices."

Use soft eyes: In some spiritual practices, people are encouraged to look upon others with soft eyes. This means looking at people with love and compassion instead of irritation and judgment. Notice how easy it is to regard teens with judgment, and then remember that what they portray superficially does not adequately inform you about who they are on a deeper level. Experiment for a day (or a lifetime) by looking upon teens (and all humanity) with soft eyes.

Check your statements: Imagine your comments to your daughter represent either bank deposits or withdrawals; how does the balance look? Deposits are positive comments while withdrawals are critical. It's easy to get overdrawn, so remember that the biggest problem with commenting too frequently on what is not working is that it results in more negativity, not less. Use self-awareness to keep your accounts in the black.

Practice appreciation: Tell your daughter often how happy you are to have a teenager. When she's funny, laugh fully. When she's clever, take a moment to really enjoy how her mind works. Both savor who she is and convey your enjoyment (often and generously) for it:

- I love having a teenager! You just keep evolving into a more amazing person, and I like being around you.

- No one makes me laugh the way you do. You always see things with a creative twist. You have a certain wicked, but brilliant, way of seeing things.

Even during tough times, you can verbalize optimism:

- Hey, I know we had a rough patch today. Even when we clunk heads, I still adore you.

Hello, hello: It's easy to get lazy about hellos and good-byes. Many teen girls are not great at basic social rituals. Instead, they are often preoccupied with feelings and struggles we may know little about. No matter her mood, commit to greeting her with love and warmth. Even the prickliest of teens will admit she needs these signs of love.

Walk your talk: If you would like her to speak in a positive tone of voice or think before acting, pay close attention to your own communication and behavior. It takes a lot of self-control and self-awareness to model the values we teach as parents. For example, teens often hear that gossip is wrong and hurtful, only to hear their parents gossip. Warning: your teen daughter can spot your hypocrisy faster than a cheetah can spot a chubby wildebeest.

We've scraped off the culturally conditioned negativity toward teens. Now let's bump up your ability to connect positively with your daughter.

2

A Crash Course on Connection

During the teen years, you'll experience many changes in family interactions. Ways of relating that used to feel natural and satisfying can be thrown off by your daughter's mood, her schedule, or her reluctance to engage. Hang in there, because the most important thing you can give your teen daughter is a strong relationship with you. While it won't be all bonding moments and heart-to-heart talks, your overall loving connection will facilitate her healthy development like nothing else can.

You May Be Noticing:

- She's in her room more—with the door closed.

- She has an endless appetite for socializing with friends, but she won't go into the grocery store with you. She'd rather sit in the car texting.

- Peaceful connection can dissolve into conflict in a second.

- Her level of activity can range from very active (no time for you or your requests) to completely inert (you fight the urge to check for a pulse).

- Feeling in the loop isn't what it used to be. She prefers to rarely consult you and becomes annoyed when you seek access to her life.

You Are Important

No matter how it seems sometimes, your teen daughter wants and needs a strong relationship with you. In fact, in 2007 the Associated Press and MTV interviewed nearly thirteen hundred young people, twelve to twenty-four years old, and found that the majority of teens find the most happiness with family and are often happier being with their parents than being with their friends. In this same Youth Happiness Study, guess who most teens listed as their heroes: parents! (Associated Press–MTV 2007). So no matter how her sharp retorts pierce you, see beyond her prickly attitude and remember that, in the big picture, you are important.

> The most important thing you can give your teen daughter is a strong relationship with you.

More good news: A YMCA parent and teen survey, "Talking with Teens," commissioned for the 2000 White House Conference on Teenagers, reported that 78 percent of teens said they turn to their parents in times of need. Teens are three times more likely than their parents to say *not having enough time together* is their biggest frustration (YMCA 2000). If you're surprised by these findings, you're not alone. The teen years can make parents question their importance.

Then and Now

Intimately connecting with your daughter as a little girl was often natural and effortless. The only challenge was how many times you could play Candy Land without losing your mind. Even tedious errands could be transformed into adventures with your bright-eyed and curious companion. Days began cuddling your warm biscuit and ended with her precious head leaving a sweaty spot on your shoulder. Even with the stress and exhaustion, many parents experience a sense of unsurpassed intimacy and love in these early years.

Now she's a teenager. Luckily this transformation has unfolded over time, so you've already made many of the necessary adjustments. For example, she doesn't appreciate that little pat on the butt you used to give her, and you can't call her Lamby-Pie in front of her friends. There are moments when she surprises you with bursts of affection followed by moments in which her scathing gaze makes you wonder if you're emitting some kind of toxic daughter-repelling pheromone. Wistfully you remember the days her entire being lit up at the mere sight of you.

Changes are everywhere, and you may feel confused about how to respond. Your once vivacious child may be sullen and withdrawn at the family gatherings that she used to love. She went from "queen" of the neighborhood to queen of solitary room confinement. And there are those strange choices she makes that you find so hard to believe: "*Really, honey?* You'd rather stay in this hot car than run into the store with me?" Yes, apparently she would.

In some ways, your daughter completely depends on you, but in others she pushes you away. While she holds your historic bond deep inside her, nurturing a relationship with you is low priority. In fact, if you've been a fairly consistent and loving parent, she has the luxury of taking you for granted. Believe it or not, this is a compliment to you.

Like generations of teens before her, your daughter is driven by two developmental tasks: cultivating identity and becoming independent. If there is a gentle, graceful way to master these foundational elements of adulthood, few parents have witnessed it. The process is crucial, not pretty. Accepting that the road will be intermittently bumpy will help you trade panic mode for resilience mode. Understanding more about her daily stresses helps you keep her moodiness in perspective.

A Day in Her Life

There are many reasons for your daughter's inconsistent moods and behavior. To better connect with her, even when she's spiraling out of control, let's take a walk through her day.

In Her Shoes

Your daughter's day is long and multifaceted. She doesn't just "go to school." She navigates emotional, social, and academic challenges from the time she wakes up until she goes to bed. You don't need to be aware of all the details—you just need to appreciate the overall struggle. As she deals with diverse challenges, she draws from coping skills that resemble an incomplete deck of cards. She rifles through the deck all day long in search of the correct card to play for the challenge at hand: talking to a teacher, navigating a misunderstanding with a friend, feeling dismissed by a romantic interest. Often she grabs the wrong card, which is hardly surprising, since developmentally she lacks a complete deck.

Since projecting attractiveness, acceptability, and normalcy are key priorities for teen girls, feelings of inadequacy are inevitable. No wonder she's touchy by the time she gets home.

No matter how upbeat and charming you are at the end of the day, her energy is crashing and you're *her "crash zone."* She's tired of projecting her ideal image. Her composure is spent, and she can be herself with you. At the mellower end of the behavioral spectrum, she may be quiet or indifferent. Some girls withdraw to their rooms to decompress.

Other teen girls seek interaction, though not necessarily pleasantly. Stressed and overstimulated, teens often fire frustration bombs onto parents or siblings, who understandably feel attacked. Whether your daughter has a predictable way of hitting the crash zone or mixes it up, remember that you are very likely t*he most important human in her life.*

Banishing the Disrespect Myth

Since your daughter is a developing adult with partially developed coping strategies, you can see her rudeness in a more productive way. While some of her coping strategies may be quite skillful and appropriate (savor those moments), others seem better labeled "coping flops." Much of her rude behavior is, in fact, *a coping flop.* For example, when you comment on her mistreatment of a sibling, a wet towel on her floor, or the chore she forgot to do, your daughter responds with a rude verbal eruption; a blank, confused, or hostile facial expression; or physical and emotional withdrawal.

Exercise: Teen Behaviors That Trigger My Perception of Disrespect

Think about the last time you felt disrespected by your daughter. List behaviors that trigger your perception of disrespect.

_____

_____

_____

Disrespect = Coping Crisis

When you feel disrespected by your daughter, try this new way of looking at her behaviors: *disrespect equals a coping crisis*. What you interpret as disrespect may actually be your daughter behaving rudely because she is overwhelmed. Coping strategies elude her. To understand this, think about the last time you were rude, short, or dismissive with someone. How clear, resourceful, empowered, and capable were you feeling in that moment? Chances are you were emotionally overwhelmed or mentally and physically exhausted. Pressures taxed your resources. Similarly, various pressures underlie your daughter's meltdowns, so it's helpful to look beyond their face value. Your reminder to pick up the towel may very well be the straw that breaks the camel's back. The point isn't that poor coping excuses rude behavior; the point is that poor coping *drives* rude behavior. Teen rudeness often has absolutely nothing to do with disrespect.

How to Deal with a Coping Crisis: Zooming Out vs. Zooming In

If your daughter's behavior reflects a coping crisis, *you can still respond*. A coping crisis is not a hall pass for rudeness. But now that you see her as a child having a coping crisis, your *response* to her behavior will be more empathic, skillful, and successful. Avoiding battle mode helps you communicate effectively, which prevents your message from being met with irate indignation.

When you feel really angry, adjust your perspective by employing this visual: Imagine you're holding a camera. Anger puts the camera on "zoom in," which means you zero in on a few details of the larger picture. For example, you zoom in on the fact that she's late, or she left a mess, or she just treated you terribly. Because you're not considering context while in zoom-in mode, your anger burns hotter. Now if you turn the imaginary lens to zoom out (easier said than done), the target of your focus softens and more context comes into view. She's late because her practice ran over; she left a mess because she overslept, and she plans to clean it up soon; she erupted because she felt you criticized her and she failed to employ better coping behavior in that moment. Again, you're not accepting the behavior as appropriate. You are reducing conflict and improving your approach by acknowledging a larger context.

> Teen rudeness often has absolutely nothing to do with disrespect.

Your mind can both zoom in and zoom out to change its focus. The ability to do both is called *cognitive flexibility*, and it's a very good skill to have. Knowing when you're zoomed in too close allows you to choose to zoom out and derive the benefit of more context. Breathing mindfully while relaxing your clenched muscles and softening your focus helps you ease your angry feelings and proceed through the challenge more skillfully.

As you integrate new skills such as cognitive flexibility into your parenting, don't despair if it takes a while to see positive results. (If you are the parent of an intense thirteen-year-old, we may be talking years here.) Even when your daughter shows you little in the moment, take pride in acting as a powerful example of how to behave well when stressed. You are also cultivating trust and infusing your relationship with goodwill.

Mood Meteorology and Teen Girls

Mood changes also let you know your daughter is struggling to cope. If you're having trouble understanding how your daughter can rapidly shift from treating you as *extremely important* to the *object of intense irritation,* think of her moods as weather. In any given day, there are many weather changes (mood changes). Some days (hours or even minutes) the weather is intense and unstable, while others days weather is mild and even pleasant. Skies can go from clear blue to stormy in the time it takes you to brush your teeth.

With teen girls, triggers stimulate abrupt changes in weather: a disappointing grade, a perceived social slight at school, an acne flare-up, learning she's been "defriended" on a social networking site. Since she may not tell you about the trigger (or even consciously realize it herself), give her the benefit of the doubt when you see a quick, dramatic weather change. She's struggling with something that compromises her ability to behave well in the moment. Stabilizing your own emotional weather patterns creates the best climate control.

Remembering Core Goodness

In the early years, you seldom lost sight of your child's core goodness. She was a love dispenser who could warm your heart as it had never been warmed before. She emanated sweetness and light. Even her shenanigans were adorable. But during these teen years, your belief in her core goodness may be put to the test. At times, you feel so exasperated by her behavior that you want to push her away or yell at her—or you may fantasize about running away from home yourself.

When behavior is skillful, kind, and appropriate, it aligns with core goodness and people feel great. When behavior is unskillful, unkind, inappropriate, and therefore out of alignment with core goodness, people feel awful. The behavior does not define the human producing it. Even wonderful, lovely humans are absolutely capable of producing horrible behavior. This is true for parents as well as teens. If you have a horrible parenting moment, it does not mean you are a horrible parent or a despicable person.

It means you're out of alignment with your core goodness. Neither your behavior nor your daughter's defines who either of you is at your core.

Remembering your teen as a young child can help you stay connected to her core goodness. Sprinkle reminders throughout your home: old photographs, art projects, or the pinch pot she made for you in kindergarten will remind you that your daughter is more than her current behavior. One parent did it this way:

> I put an old photo of my daughter from second grade on the inside of my kitchen cabinet. Every morning when I get my coffee, I see her toothless grin smiling at me. It stings a little to see that picture because I'm having a really hard time with her right now. I struggle with taking all her behavior personally. Anyway, when I look at that picture, I remember who she really is at her core and remind myself that this difficult phase will get better.

Reflecting on sweet memories helps you remember the positive feelings you have about your daughter. Circulating positive feelings is beneficial because it realigns core goodness, both your daughter's and your own. The positive feelings will infuse your connection with your daughter, stoking the potential for positive connection. Teen girls can be both oblivious as well as psychically attuned to parental feelings, so readjusting your feelings might just show results in your next interaction.

Exercise: Reclaiming Positive Feelings

To help you keep in touch with the positive feelings, jot down several memories of your daughter that make you smile.

_____

_____

_____

Exercise: Memories I Have of Myself That Create Positive Feelings

Since parenting teen girls can take a toll on how you feel about yourself, it's helpful to reflect on your own positive memories. Breathe into the positive feelings and allow them to bolster your commitment to seeing and feeling your own core goodness. Record a few memories below:

_____

_____

_____

Keep Your Eyes on the Prize

At the end of the day, your daughter has experimented with many different behaviors and identities. They come and go naturally, without heavy intervention from you. And though some may be more desirable than others, through them all you want your daughter to know she is deeply valued and loved. You want her to understand that your relationship with her is more important than the behavior she exhibited. No matter how it appears, she needs a strong relationship with you. Beyond the realm of her behavior, you want her (and you) to connect with her core goodness.

If your daughter participates in seriously risky behaviors, it is even more crucial to remember her core goodness. Many parents are so scared, upset, and mad about risky behaviors that they punish their teen by withdrawing all signs of love. This is a very risky behavior of a different sort; avoid it at all costs! Your daughter needs your love even more when she's blowing it. Deal with the behavior, but stay committed to loving your child. And remember that most teens make it through very rough times and reclaim qualities and the core goodness from which they have strayed.

Be a Curious Explorer of Behavior

Parents often ask me, "Am I supposed to disregard my teen's unacceptable behavior just because it's developmentally appropriate?" The answer is no. When she was four, it was developmentally appropriate for her to hit and push when angry, but you didn't accept the behavior just because it was normal for her age. The trick is to deal with behavior that is unacceptable without losing her (or your) connection to her core goodness. You want to convey that the behavior is of concern and that you still love and believe in her.

If you explore the behavior that concerns you instead of getting lost in conflict, you'll have more resources to work as a team *with* your daughter *against* the problem. In contrast, if you withdraw or fight mercilessly with her about the behavior, you won't address the problem and you will injure the relationship. Without you on her side, the problem can get worse. If your relationship is injured because conflict smothers exploration and batters connection, she may get better at hiding her behavior and fail to identify you as a resource.

Gather Information

Depending on what she's up to, your nerves may be getting a real workout. Here's what to do: feel your feelings, write them down, share them with a friend, cry, breathe, go to kickboxing/meditation/yoga, and read chapter 3, Self-Care for Sanity. Refrain from spewing your fear and anger onto your daughter.

> Your daughter needs your love even more when she's blowing it.

Instead of conveying your fear and anger, come from a nonthreatening, nonhostile, caring place and make inquiries about her concerning behavior. *Teen girls respond much better to inquiries than assumptions.* In fact, assuming the worst about them often triggers them into exploring the worst, since no one expects better of them anyway. Let her know you care about her, and that part of your job as her parent is to guide her behavior. If she's not completely open, and you don't get all the information you desire, don't despair. Your daughter will still get the message that you care more about *her* than about punishing her. As she experiences your concern, instead of your accusations, she will learn to trust you as an ally.

Crucial Connecting

Chapter 4 contains many tips for effective communication. However, because communication is crucial to your positive connection with your daughter, I will briefly address it here as well.

Win-Win Scripts

You can improve your connection with your teen with win-win scripts. A *win-win script* allows both you and your daughter to feel like winners in a conversation that produces good results. One or more of these elements will help you create a win-win interaction with your daughter:

1. Neutrally describe the issue.

2. Acknowledge your teen's intention/goal.

3. Speak to her core goodness.

4. Clarify the preferred behavior needed.

Think about how you can include these elements in conversations with your daughter. Using them will help keep the communication lines open. They respect both your needs and hers, and help you move together toward workable solutions to problem behavior. Here are a few examples:

BALANCING COMMITMENTS

o You've always been such a good and kind friend, and I want you to get plenty of time to socialize. We need to find a balance between social time with friends and family time.

○ I respect how devoted you are to your school work; however, I still need you to clear your dinner dishes and wipe down the counters.

BEING RESPECTFUL AND RESPONSIBLE

○ I want to give you more and more freedom. You're an adventurer and I love that about you. You need to do your part by checking in when I ask you to and being home on time. I know we can get this right so we're both satisfied.

○ I love your spontaneity. It's one of the reasons you're so fun. I know it's not always easy to keep me in the loop when your plans change. Here's the deal: if you want freedom, you need to keep me posted.

○ I appreciate the thinking you've put into why I should say yes. I love the way your mind works and will try to say yes as much as I can. This time, however, the answer is no. I'm sorry you're disappointed.

○ I appreciate that your room is your space. I want you to have your own space, and I want to honor your need for privacy. My need is for you to keep clothes off the floor. I don't feel good about buying clothes that live on the floor and, for me, putting them away feels respectful. I know other moms have different standards, but this is mine and I'd like you to work with me.

DEALING WITH RISKY BEHAVIOR

○ I think you're really smart, and I don't want to offend you by telling you this. I know you love and trust your friends and would never want to create conflict with them. However, if one of your friends has been drinking and plans to drive, you need to stop it, even if you have to get other people involved. I want you to call me or someone you trust, but never, ever get into a car with someone who has been drinking, even if it's an adult.

○ Taking risks is part of being a teenager. You are such a wonderful person, and I love and adore you no matter how hard things get. I'm concerned that you are taking risks that could endanger your life. I'm curious about what you're dealing with and how you feel about it.

TAKING CARE OF YOURSELF

○ I hear that you don't feel tired until midnight. You're becoming so responsible that I want to back off and let you make the call. But if you're not getting at least nine hours of sleep, I'll need to step in and be a bigger pain about this issue. It's critical to your health and learning that you get the recommended sleep for your age.

○ I know you're not a fan of breakfast. Make me a list of what you can stand eating, and I'll do everything I can to work with you on this. Skipping breakfast isn't an option, but choosing from lots of possibilities is.

Exercise: Write a Win-Win Script

Now create a win-win script for you and your daughter, following the four steps below:

1. Neutrally describe the issue.

_____

_____

2. Acknowledge the teen's intention/goal.

_____

_____

3. Speak to her core goodness.

_____

_____

4. Clarify the needed behavior.

_____

_____

Remember, your job is to recognize your teen's core goodness and nourish your relationship. She may be open and honest or she might shut you down. You can control only your part of the relationship. Stick to your commitment and be the best parent you can be, no matter how she handles her role. If she seems stubborn and uncooperative, you're still planting seeds that will create growth in her future.

The Importance of Small Moments

Connection with your daughter may come in a variety of small moments scattered throughout the day and week. If you're not getting big stretches of time together, don't sweat it. Think small. Increments of just a few, sweet minutes do count, especially when you are undistracted and truly present. Here are some ideas from real teen girls:

○ My dad makes my waffle in the morning, and he toasts it just right. Then he hangs out with me for a while before he leaves for work.

○ My mom texts me sometimes to wish me good luck on a test.

○ My dad and I watch football together.

○ My granny makes me hot chocolate in a mug she got for me. She made a rule that no one gets to use that mug but me.

○ My mom reads her book in my room while I do my homework sometimes. It makes me feel less isolated and lonely. Even though we're both doing different stuff, I like her company.

Exercise: Small Things I Will Do to Connect with My Daughter

Now it's your turn to think of small ways to connect with your daughter. If you're not sure where to start, look to things you used to do when she was little and consider trying some again. If you used to read to her and she's currently up to her ears in US history, offer to read a few pages aloud to her.

_____

_____

_____

_____

More Ways to Enhance Connection

Because connecting with your daughter is good for both of you, watch for ways to enhance your connection with her. Here are a few additional ideas:

Catch your bee with honey: You know how you experience your daughter's tone, facial expressions, and mood, but do you know how she experiences yours? Take a moment occasionally to see yourself, your behavior, your tone, your mood, and your interactions from her perspective. Some parents notice how barky they are or preoccupied with the many tasks of everyday life. Others become aware of time spent on their cell phone or personal computer.

"Think teen": You will increase opportunities to connect if you sharpen your ability to "think teen." Pay attention to ways your daughter may be open to connecting. Here are some ideas from real parents:

o I've learned to recognize when my daughter is trying to connect with me. The other day, she wanted to share a song she downloaded from the computer and I was busy, so I almost waved her off. Then I realized this is an invitation! I stopped what I was doing, which was really hard, and listened to the song with her. It was just a five-minute interaction, but that is what I'm learning to value and be available for.

o My daughter is most accessible late in the evenings when I am most exhausted. I find a reason to visit her in her room to create a small connection before bed. She's not much of a talker but likes a cup of tea and a good-night hug.

Take advantage of unexpected opportunities: If your daughter is sick, injured, or feels out of place and self-conscious at a family social event, connect spontaneously. You will find she's extremely open to you. Tap into a sense of fun and make the most of her accessibility. Here are some connections teens have appreciated:

o When I was stranded at home with a sprained ankle, my dad got my old Legos out of storage. I thought he was ridiculous, but I was so bored I started building a kingdom with him. We used to do that when I was little.

o Every year my family has a giant family reunion. I'm kind of shy and get totally overwhelmed by all of the hugging and socializing. My mom tries to rescue me from certain relatives, and we hang out and have fun.

Don't accidentally penalize her: When my older teen comes out of her room, I often have an impulse to remind her to take out the garbage. Ooops! What message does that send? It's better for her to stay in her room! To avoid negatively penalizing girls, we can leave sticky notes on their doors reminding them of chores and tasks. When they emerge from their private spaces, we can be mindful to keep their experience positive.

Now that you have some great ideas about how to enhance your connection with your daughter, we need to make a U-turn to check out your connection to your own health. Teen girls aren't the only ones going through developmental changes. In order to feel your best while doing your best, you need to breathe life into your own health and well-being.

3

Self-Care for Sanity

If you're like a lot of parents, the harder time your teen daughter is having, the harder time you're having. The saying "Parents can only be as happy as their unhappiest child" strikes a chord of recognition. If you feel as if things are just too busy to take care of yourself, pay close attention to this chapter and the exercises designed to boost your self-care. Small changes now have the power to create great results in all aspects of your life.

You May Be Noticing:

- ○ You feel exhausted a lot of the time.

- ○ You look forward to your semiannual teeth cleaning as an opportunity to lie down and relax.

- ○ You question your mood and memory more often than you used to.

- ○ Spacing out to TV represents your best stab at self-care.

- ○ You can't remember the last thing you did to really treat yourself. You suspect it involved an ill-advised food choice.

- You hear yourself say, "Things are just really busy right now" way too often.

- You assume you'll resurrect your friendships and love life "when things slow down a little."

Healthy Separation

It's very common for parents to feel overwhelmed by the challenges of raising teen girls. When we don't take time to nourish our own health, friendships, and interests, we risk emotionally collapsing into the lives of our daughters. Some parents say:

- My daughter is so intense. On her bad days, I feel like her hostage.

- I feel heartbroken when my daughter struggles. I have trouble separating my mood from hers.

- My daughter's attitude affects the whole family. I resent how powerfully she impacts the family mood.

Part of self-care is cultivating a sense of healthy separation. When you nourish your own life, you will feel less emotionally vacuumed into your daughter's moods. You'll be able to see yourself as an anchor while she's a sailboat bobbing on turbulent seas. Instead of tumbling on deck, you'll feel grounded and stable. As the anchor, you'll remain separate yet connected.

Some parents don't feel anchored; they feel they're missing the boat entirely. If you feel this way, please be assured that, by the time you finish this book, you'll have the skills and information you need to increase healthy connection in all of your relationships. Many factors create disconnection and alienation in families: conflict, divorce, trauma, loss, addiction, and mental illness. Even without such factors, many parents feel hurt and sidelined as their teen daughters become more involved with friends and less with family. Without getting mired in

> When you nourish your own life, you will feel less emotionally vacuumed into your daughter's moods.

frustration, guilt, blame, or regret, seek to create more healthy connection in your life. Start with your own balanced self-care, which will, in turn, energize a better relationship with your daughter.

Your Teen's Impact on You—and How to Deal with It

You've probably noticed that your daughter isn't the only one on the roller coaster. In a study of more than two hundred teens and their families, researchers found that parents experience big changes in their own lives when their children hit puberty (Steinberg and Steinberg 1994). It turns out that midlife crisis has less to do with the age of the adult than with the age of the oldest child in a family. Midlife distress is often set off by the oldest child entering adolescence. Marital satisfaction reaches an all-time low when the oldest child hits the teen years. On the upside, couples that stay together report an increase in marital satisfaction in postteen years. Whether parents are married or single, Steinberg and Steinberg's research shows a parent's happiness influences the quality of parent-teen interaction.

Taking care of yourself strengthens your resistance to the stresses of the teen years. It also reduces your susceptibility to those parental moments that we'd all rather not talk about.

Bad Parent Hangover

Let's face it, parenting a teen girl isn't easy, and we all have moments we're not proud of. My personal experience as the mother of two teen girls, combined with my private practice work, led me to discover the *bad parent hangover*, the painful emotional aftermath that lingers after a parental meltdown. Some parents yell, some cry, some throw full-blown tantrums. A defining feature is lack of emotional control. Busy parents lacking healthy balance are at high risk to impulsively react in challenging moments. Instead of responding skillfully, we react from weariness, hurt, impatience, or hostility.

While many things lie beyond parental control—the weather, the economy, your daughter's mood—creating self-care does not. You have the ability to initiate and maintain a practice of solid self-care that benefits *everyone*. Taking care of yourself is a necessity, not a luxury. It gives you the energy to be the happiest and most effective person and parent you can be.

Changing the Scene

Most parents can easily note the regular stressors that turn a good day into a bad movie. For you and your daughter, it might be mornings before school, when stress levels are high and time is scarce. Or maybe it's during homework—or those dreaded moments before you tell your daughter, "No, you can't do that." During these times, it's easy to stumble into heated scenes you'd rather avoid. Try using the Changing the Scene technique to rewrite them. The exercise below will show you how.

Exercise: Changing the Scene

Find a few minutes and a quiet space. Take your time with each step. Breathe deeply and bring to mind as much detail as possible.

1. Imagine one of your stress-trigger situations.

2. Instead of your typical reaction, imagine yourself feeling calm and effective.

3. Imagine words coming out of your mouth that are intelligent, focused, and productive. What would you say?

4. With as much detail as possible, imagine feeling, sounding, and responding exactly as you'd like to. The more vividly you can imagine these positive changes in your mind and feel them in your body, the more your brain will generate the neural pathways and networks to help you actualize in "real life" what you rehearse mentally.

The next time you encounter one of your stress-trigger situations, breathe deeply and tap into your rewrite of the scene. If your daughter acts from a different script, remember you have control only of yourself, and stick to your part.

Taking Inventory

We all squirm when thinking about our bad parenting moments. For me, they're especially embarrassing considering my immersion in the topic of teen girl development. As we raise our teen girls, most of us will have parenting moments we wouldn't want captured on a smart phone and posted on YouTube! To strike a balance, we must also create and acknowledge our *good* parenting moments. The exercise below will help you reflect on those moments. Like teen girls, we parents can be our best when we generate and sustain positive feelings about ourselves.

Exercise: Good Parent Inventory

Write a quick inventory that reflects things you know you do *well* as a parent. Acknowledge big acts or small, subtle offerings. If you do a great job getting your daughter to her many commitments on time, write that down. If you're great at walking the line between supporting her and letting her make her own mistakes, note that now. If you're gifted at tuning in to her feelings, put that on your list. Remind yourself that all of your efforts are an expression of love that benefit you and your daughter.

My Inventory of Strengths

_____

_____

_____

You Are the Well

Think of yourself as a well. The more water in the well, the more energy and personal resources you have to meet life's demands. When your self-care is strong and consistent, you fill the well with energy and personal resources that boost your overall mood and vitality. You'll think more flexibly, creatively, and intelligently. You'll face challenges with goodwill and patience.

Doesn't it also make sense that watching *you* manage stress and make time for yourself is the best way to teach stress management and self-care to your daughter? You aren't just a parent to your teen daughter—you are her sample adult. When you lead by example, teen girls pay attention. Often inclined to tune out what you *say*, they absorb a lot about *how* you live life.

> By boosting your self-care, you show your daughter (while reminding yourself) that life can be fun.

Too often parents unintentionally make life look like a drag. While teens whine about homework, chores, siblings, and other annoyances, adults often whine about traffic, bills, and the unrelenting messes we clean up. Teens observe that it doesn't seem fun to be an adult. They question all the hoop jumping. They think, *I'm doing all of this just to become a stressed-out, bill-paying, mess-cleaning grump? Whatever!* By boosting your self-care, you show your daughter (while reminding yourself) that life can be fun.

Teen Girls Say:

○ My mom started taking salsa lessons. She comes home all happy and dancing around.

○ My dad goes to meditation every Wednesday night. It's made him way more chill and easygoing. We want him to go more!

○ My dad was out of work for over a year, and his depression made everyone in my family miserable. Then he started mountain biking with a neighbor, which made life better for all of us.

Prioritizing your own happiness and continued growth transforms both you and your daughter. As you enjoy your own life more, she sees it can be cool to become an adult. When you put yourself on your to-do list, you experience a lift in energy and mood that flows into all areas of your life.

Getting Started

What can you give yourself to improve your self-care? Is there an activity you've been curious about? Yoga? Pottery? Art? Mountain biking? Hiking? Meditation? Book club? Piano lessons? Martial arts?

Parents Say:

- It's always piqued my interest when I see people kayaking.

- I've heard a lot about the benefits of meditation and am kind of curious about taking a class or getting a CD.

- I've always wanted to take an art class but just never seem to make it happen.

Exercise: New Activities I Would Like to Try

Think of some activities you would like to try to improve your self-care, and list them below.

_____

_____

_____

Exercise: Reconnecting with Past Activities

If you're having trouble coming up with compelling new activities, try reconnecting with an activity from your past. For example, if you loved swimming, playing an instrument, or camping, reclaiming that activity will feel like a homecoming. Just be patient with yourself until you hit your flow with it again. List some activities you'd like to reclaim.

_____

_____

_____

If you are motivated to connect with one or several activities right away, go for it. If not, be easy with yourself. Warm up slowly by taking microsteps.

Microsteps to Sanity

When taking action seems daunting, think small, because small efforts create momentum. To get started, research your interest and find information about local resources. You can also visit a local resource, such as the parks and recreation department in your city. You might end up chatting with someone about the activity, which generates even more momentum.

Next, identify ways to schedule your activity. What can you remove from your schedule to make room for your self-care? (You may find this step very difficult because everything looks so important.) Write your self-care activity *on your calendar*— treat your self-care commitment with the same respect that you treat other commitments.

Now get excited about your plan. Make sure you have what you need. Share your enthusiasm with people, or talk to people who are already doing the activity. Finally, just show up! We can think about what we should do or want to do until the cows come home. Ultimately it's about showing up. When parents make this breakthrough, they say things such as "I can't believe I waited so long!" *and* "How did I get along without this?" People never regret taking proper care of themselves.

Here's a tip*:* If you are overscheduled now, say no to new commitments unless they represent self-care or something of absolute importance. Saying no protects you from burnout and gives you space to say yes to yourself.

TAKE A MICROSTEP RIGHT NOW

Copy a few of your self-care ideas onto a piece of paper and post it on the fridge. Let your family know you're working on expanding your self-care. Ask for their support, and let them know your improved health and happiness will be good for them too. This assignment has three primary benefits:

1. It keeps you accountable. Seeing that list every day reminds you of your commitment.

2. It rallies support. You've now involved other people who will ask about your interests. Note: Respond directly to any initial teasing by stating clearly that you want support or silence.

3. It models health for everyone in the family. Other family members may follow your lead.

Once you develop good self-care habits, family life will go more smoothly for everyone.

PARENTS SHARE THEIR MICROSTEPS

Small efforts toward self-care can be even more crucial in very stressful times:

○ When my daughter was going through a really scary period of experimentation and defiance, I gave up a lot to be on call for the next crisis. I learned to work with my stress by practicing breathing techniques and being kind to myself in small ways. Even little things like taking a bath or fixing a really healthy, delicious meal became key to my stress survival.

○ Money has been tight lately. I'm taking the edge off my stress by working on my yard. Gardening relaxes me and it costs nothing. It takes my mind off my worries, and making the yard look good gives me a feeling of accomplishment.

○ When I feel burned out, I tend to forget the small things that make me feel better. Remembering to put music on, call friends, and walk my dog around the block make a difference.

Exercise: Keep it Simple

Name some small steps you can take to manage difficult times:

_____

_____

_____

Avoiding Pseudo Self-Care

If you feel even small steps are impossible, you may be vulnerable to pseudo self-care behaviors. Pseudo self-care behaviors *seem* rejuvenating or relaxing at first because they offer a sense of pleasure or relief. Over time, these behaviors threaten health instead of boosting health. Pseudo self-care behaviors include these:

○ Spending too much

○ Having affairs or inappropriate relationships

○ Abusing street or prescription drugs

○ Drinking too much

○ Eating too much

Remember, *numbing behaviors aren't nurturing behaviors*. Nurturing behaviors enhance your health and well-being. Numbing behaviors create additional problems and ultimately more stress.

If you are engaged in any of the above behaviors, find a support group and/or make an appointment with a therapist to get confidential support. You are worth the investment of time and energy. In the big picture, you want to replace pseudo self-care with healthy self-care. Healthy self-care supports feeling good without injuring your body, your heart, your finances, or your loved ones.

How to Pursue Therapy

Many people ask around, or chose a therapist after hearing a friend, family member, or colleague talk about their experience with one. Others contact clergy or look online or in the phone book for mental health services available in their area. If you have mental health benefits through your health insurance, find out what providers are approved and what coverage is provided.

Once you have chosen and talked with your therapist, you'll know after one or two sessions if the therapist is a good fit for you. Remember, *you are the consumer*. Don't be afraid to try a different therapist if you don't feel a good fit with the first one.

Keeping Your Well Full

Now that you're putting water *in* your well with your new self-care skills, you'll want to avoid unnecessary leaks and drainage. To avoid drainage with your teen girl, find a way to love and support her without feeling triggered into anger, fear, hurt, or confusion. Learning to create healthy separation from your daughter's moods and behaviors is vital to your parental skill and well-being.

During challenging moments, the more emotionally overwhelmed or out of control you feel, the more fused you are with the problem and not the solution. As you know, this just makes things worse. Take care of yourself and your emotional state so that you can shift into a solution orientation.

Teen Development Creates Stress for Parents

Did you know that driving you nuts is part of your daughter's healthy development? When she picks on you, avoids you, argues with you, criticizes you, teases you, laughs at you, ignores you, blows up at you, or in other ways *grinds your last nerve to paste,* she's working on mastering two crucial developmental tasks: gaining independence and developing her identity. We touched on these briefly in chapter 2, but let's explore them more deeply now, because understanding them will help you care for yourself while parenting your daughter.

TEEN TASK 1: GAINING INDEPENDENCE

Your daughter needs to push away and be less close to you. Yes, you can be an important and stabilizing force for her. No, she isn't super interested in you, your feelings, or your life. She mostly doesn't consider the impact she has on you. And when you feel the need to share your feelings, you may be greeted by a decided lack of enthusiasm. Every now and again she may "beam in" to share, connect, compliment, or criticize, but for the most part she focuses her attention elsewhere.

If being her parent has been your main source of identity and value, her need to separate will be extremely painful. It's therefore very important that you take this chapter on self-care seriously and allocate energy back into your own life and personal development. If you resist, you'll grasp your daughter tightly in order to maintain your parental identity—only to see her recoil from you.

When your daughter pulls back from you, she's not being cruel. Her reaction is natural, age appropriate, and healthy. In fact, if your daughter doesn't recoil but instead tries to accommodate your need for her, she may sacrifice her own healthy development. She may be more attuned to your needs than her own, and such accommodation has a price. Acting as emotional caretaker for a parent requires sacrifice from a teen girl, who should be developing a sense of herself as separate from Mom or Dad. Although this can be a father-daughter dynamic, it is more common between mothers and daughters.

> Did you know that driving you nuts is part of your daughter's healthy development?

What's the bottom line? Teen girls don't want to be emotional guardians for their parents. They don't want to meet our emotional needs so that we can feel warm and fuzzy about ourselves. They don't want to give advice on whom parents date or how parents should handle personal problems. They are driven by a biological mandate to create the separateness they need to become adults. Now that your daughter is a teen, healthy, effective parenting involves allowing her to need you less. A typical course is for your daughter to need you less in general, punctuated by spasms of desperately needing (or demanding) your help or attention: *"Daaaad!!! I forgot my book at school and now I'm going to get a zero on my homework and you need to help me now!"*

When you learn to be available while also letting go, you enjoy the payoff: she won't perceive you as needy or lacking a life. When you support her separation process and also develop yourself and your own life, you make it interesting and emotionally comfortable for her to circle back around to connect with you.

TEEN TASK 2: DEVELOPING IDENTITY

It's been years since your daughter declared she will marry you when she grows up. She now denies ever vowing to live with you forever and ever. Just as her early identity was based on being close to you and *similar* to you, her teen identity involves bending away from you (and some of your values) toward her peer culture. She needs to identify with her social circle in order to create her identity.

You go from being the "star" of her universe to being the rain on her parade. How can she create a unique identity if she's a pea in your pod? Her teasing, ignoring, and articulation of your numerous flaws help her see herself as *different* from you because (apparently) you are often lame, embarrassing, and overall ridiculous. Instead of taking her behavior personally, see her as needing to devalue you so she can feel big and independent. When she was two, she walked around saying, *"No!"* and *"Mine!"* and you were able to giggle, knowing she was working on boundaries, power, and seeing herself as a separate entity. Guess what? Here you have the same scenario, only minus the diapers.

When you refrain from taking your daughter's behavior personally, you resist blurting out things like "Wow, if you treat your friends the way you treat me, you won't have any friends!" There's no benefit in lash-outs; they model poor impulse control—

which you need to save for the really, really bad days! Unless she has big social problems, your daughter definitely treats her friends better; that's typical for this developmental stage. When you remember her underlying developmental tasks, you will be able to observe her behavior without becoming her victim. This is leak control for your well.

More Tips to Keep Water in Your Well

The more ways you can develop to keep water in your well, the more sane you'll feel and the more effective you'll be as a parent. Here are a few more tips:

Respond more, react less. Responding is grounded in emotional control. When you respond, you focus on the actual issue instead of a flare of intense feeling. Reacting is quick, impulsive, and emotionally turbocharged. Choosing to respond requires that you pause, breathe, access your sound thinking, and address the issue at hand.

Scan your body. Stress tends to nestle in the body. People vary in how they manifest its physical symptoms. When you are in a stressful moment, work with your body to decrease that stress. Get into a habit of mentally scanning your body to identify and relax areas of tension:

- Are you a jaw clencher? If so, notice when you're clenching, and loosen your jaw, relax your face, soften your expression.

- Do you contract your shoulders? If so, loosen them up and gently roll them back.

- Shake out or loosen up parts of your body that are tensing and contracting.

Spend time thoroughly identifying your body's responses to stress. Working with your body in a stressful moment promotes a healthy shift that supports you in addressing the issue at hand more effectively.

Breathe mindfully. After you've completed a body scan, focus on your breathing. Take a deep breath by inhaling slowly and evenly to the count of six. Then exhale to a slow and even count of six. Practice these slow inhales and exhales for as little as two minutes. You will notice a fast and dramatic decrease in your stress level. Honestly, relief can be this simple! I could go on and on about cortisol levels dropping and all the other benefits of mindful breathing. Better yet, why don't we skip that while you try it for yourself right now?

In this case, breathing is believing. Create a habit of practicing mindful breathing throughout your day. Anchor it to something you already do—such as driving the car, unloading the dishwasher, or watering the lawn—so you'll remember. Not only will you reduce your stress, you will also notice that you feel more serene while engaging in those activities.

Keep a sense of humor. Laughter keeps the water level of your well stable. Fortunately most girls have an enormous capacity for humor during their teen years. The sophistication of new brain development, paired with a fresh way of viewing life, can make your daughter howlingly funny. Fully enjoy her unique perceptions and allow her creativity to inspire and entertain you. Let her know you find her hilarious.

You're already on your way to creating better self-care. Completing this chapter has, I hope, stirred some ideas you can integrate into your routine. Just remember, taking care of yourself is essential and funds your ability to generate love and goodness in every aspect of your life. Just as your garden, pets, clients, and family need love and attention to flourish, so do you! Do a little something for yourself right now.

4

Talking with Teens

It takes a certain fearlessness to converse with teen girls. Exhausted, moody, or distracted, teen girls present a conversational hit-to-miss ratio that intimidates even the chattiest adults. Parents and other adults admit to feeling awkward or unsure about how to successfully engage teen girls in conversation, which holds them back from making attempts. On one hand, parents want to feel connected, offer support, and hear about their daughter's life. On the other, they feel wary of rejection and inadequacy. Since adults prefer to avoid such feelings, they often accept minimal conversation with teen girls.

You May Be Noticing:

o Your teen daughter stops a perfectly good conversation, even when it's going well. It's disorienting how quickly she can go from not talking, to talking, to indicating clearly that talking is now OVER.

o She argues with you—a lot. Even simple interactions can become heated quickly.

o Her verbalizations to you often come in the form of "microcomments" regarding characteristics (mostly flaws) you never knew you had.

- She prefers much of your communication to be delivered in brief sound bites.

- She accuses you of repeating yourself, overexplaining, and nagging, yet if you don't, the garbage overflows, the dog goes hungry, and her backpack lingers on the couch.

Talking to You Is Important

Believe it or not, talking to you is very important to your daughter. This may surprise you, just as it did author Mimi Doe when she interviewed fifteen hundred teens and asked, "What do you wish your parents did differently?" Overwhelmingly teens said they wanted their parents to *listen* to them more often. They didn't say they wanted their parents to offer solutions or advice, they simply wanted to feel heard and respected (Doe 2004). We parents need to remember how important we are, especially in light of conversations like this:

You: So what's your plan tonight?

Your daughter: Oh, I'm not sure yet.

You: Will you be having dinner at home?

Your daughter: (*now walking away*) Uhhh…yeah, maybe. I think so…

You: (*now following her*) You mentioned bringing some girls over to spend the night. Is that still happening?

Your daughter: Uhhhh…well Jade might…after she does this thing for her mom…but Emme has play practice, and Miranda hasn't texted me back yet.

You: So…when do you think you'll know?

Your daughter: MOM! CHILL! DOES EVERYTHING HAVE TO BE PLANNED OUT? I DON'T KNOW! DON'T ASK ME ANY MORE QUESTIONS!

When conversations like this occur, it can be hard to remember the bottom line: your daughter wants to talk and be heard by you. You are her *"all-important listener."* Doing a good job with this role can be especially difficult when conversations with her come with a surprise on/off switch that only she controls. It's not a power trip for her but rather a sign of her undeveloped ability to handle stress while verbalizing with you. Teen girls can feel pressure from our most reasonable questions and judgment from our most benign comments. Often they are unaware they've shut us down in midsyllable, so while we experience the switch to "off" as abrupt, they are consumed by an instinctive effort to decrease internal stress. Rather than the intended target, parents are collateral damage.

Effective Communication

To move beyond frustration or intimidation, start by accepting that teen girls will not always engage in conversation upon your invitation. A classic example is after-school pickup. When you greet her with your cheeriest "Hi, Honey, how was your day?," your teen daughter may respond in surly grunts and/or reluctant monosyllables. This is actually quite typical, so resist the urge to become offended or to make comments like "Why don't you ever talk to me?" or "Someone's grumpy…" While tempting, acting out in this way only escalates withdrawal. Instead, try saying, "After a long day, I'm sure you need some time to decompress," or "Let's get you home where you can relax for a while." Then let go of your check-in and travel in silence or with music.

Quiet time is restorative for teen girls, who are in a state of overstimulation much of the time. Your ability to tolerate and support silence reflects an attunement to your daughter's needs that enhances your connection, even when you're not talking.

Emotional Attunement

Emotional attunement means adjusting your emotional dial setting to meet the needs of your daughter's emotional space. It involves reading cues in her emotional presentation and adjusting your personal energy to complement and allow for her emotional experience. For example, if she's exhausted, your energy can be gentle and nondemanding. If she's upset and verbalizing, your energy can be receptive and attentive. If she's anxious and overwhelmed, your energy can be calm and reassuring.

When parents are not too busy or distracted, these attunements are natural and intuitive. Unfortunately most parents are also overstimulated, which means emotional attunement is harder to access and offer. It means you will need to practice clearing your own stress in order to gently transfer your focus to her. Get a sense of how she appears and sounds. You may receive explicit information from her about how she's doing, or you may need to rely on your observation skills and intuition in order to achieve attunement. You don't have to hold a high level of attunement for hours, but if you can give your daughter special priority at significant junctures, you will both go on to other responsibilities feeling greater well-being and enhanced connection.

To be emotionally attuned, you don't need to feel what your daughter feels. You don't need to fix, judge, fight with, trivialize, or strongly react to it. In fact, to be emotionally attuned, you need to resist all of that. Instead you *open and soften* both your mind and your heart, which creates a state of emotional attunement. Your ability to practice emotional attunement means that your personal dial setting allows for whatever is going on with your daughter in the moment, providing her with the feeling you are connected and caring.

Feeling "Felt"

As one teen girl put it, "I don't want advice from my parents. I just want them to kind of, you know, get it." When you offer emotional attunement to your daughter, she feels less alone in her realm of feelings and experiences because, even though you don't necessarily know all the gritty details, she feels you *feel* her. Feeling felt occurs in the subtle realm of interaction; it can be created in small nuances rather than big acts. It's nodding when she's venting. It's being available but not too close. It's listening without judging or inserting all the brilliant things you could say. It's having a loving but light and considerate touch with her based on the energy of the moment.

Knowing that someone *feels* you (understands, loves, and accepts you) is powerful, healing, and soothing. Teen girls need soothing! They have really intense lives with multiple challenges. Driving your daughter from point A to point B, listening to whatever she has to say with your heart, allowing for long silences while emanating appreciation of her journey through life, is one of the absolute best gifts you can give her. More than what you do for her, it involves how you're willing to *be* with her. Teen girls who feel "felt" by key adults tend to make it through challenges *much better* than girls who lack such attunement. Here are some attunement ideas shared by parents:

○ I'm going to try to be more present when she downloads her day. I tend to be more managerial with her than emotionally attuned. I spend so much time trying to keep her on track that I miss the whole attunement thing.

○ I'm going to let her be quiet and grumpy without making it about me. I've had trouble with that and it never ends well. She stays grumpy plus we end up in a fight.

○ My wife tells me our daughters avoid talking to me because I go into lecture mode. I'm going to try to listen more and talk less.

> Teen girls who feel "felt" by key adults tend to make it through challenges much better than girls who lack such attunement.

Take some time to think about how you can improve emotional attunement with your daughter. The exercise below will guide you.

Exercise: Improving Emotional Attunement

What will help you practice better emotional attunement with your daughter? First, identify what keeps you from being more attuned. For example, one parent said, "Having my other kids around and too much to do!"

What gets in the way of your attunement?

_____

_____

_____

In thinking about ways she could become more emotionally attuned to her daughter, the same parent said, "I need to get my daughter alone for a little bit every day so I can give her my undivided attention. I will make it really count by practicing an open and soft focus on her and anything she feels like sharing."

List some ways you can practice better attunement.

_____

_____

_____

Self-Control

The mercurial moods of teen girls can be very challenging. When your self-control is strong and you have solid ways of coping, you're able to resist flaring up at her. In trying moments, take a deep breath before you *respond*, not *react*. Keep a light hand. Remind yourself you don't need to change anything about your daughter's emotional state. You just need to be around in a steady, caring way.

The ability to control oneself in the face of stress is a huge component to healthy self-esteem, something we all want for our daughters. Our most compelling lessons are taught by example, so modeling self-control is the best way to teach it and support self-esteem. In moments when you lose self-control by yelling or taking your reaction too far, clean it up quickly with your daughter by apologizing and being fully accountable. People who apologize appropriately and generously have less long-running conflict in their lives, so this is another great skill to model for your daughter. As an adult, all of these practices will help her thrive in relationships!

Guidelines for Good Talks

Here's the major "do" when conversing with your teen: empty your mind of your parenting opinions, judgments, fears, and agendas. Dr. Daniel Siegel, codirector of the

UCLA Mindfulness Awareness Center and author of *Mindful Brain*, suggests the acronym COAL: curious, open, accepting, and loving (2007).

A leader in the area of research called "interpersonal neurobiology," Siegel presents compelling brain research suggesting the essential need for parents to increase their ability to experience *resonant awareness*, which means focusing exclusively on what is occurring in the moment purely and openly (Siegel 2007). While well-intended parents jump to embrace this suggestion, actually creating resonant awareness in your relationships requires a deep commitment of love and self-control. In time, it will replace your previous more reactive, less mindful style, and it will feel easy, natural, and deeply fulfilling.

The Beauty of COAL

As a psychologist, I like to float the words *curious*, *open*, *accepting* through my mind as I listen. No one can fix anyone else's problems. The best any of us can do is create a state of "beingness" that offers emotional safety and connection, which fosters, in turn, an atmosphere that welcomes creative thinking and optimistic collaboration. The words "curious, open, accepting, and loving" function as a mental marinade that can help us all to achieve emotional attunement and resonant awareness.

> Good listening correlates with a relaxed body, smooth breathing, and physical openness.

When you look at your daughter through this lens, you give her more than advice. You give her emotional connection and a sense of safety in opening up to you. You may not agree with what she's saying or the way she says it. Your commitment to suspending judgment and avoiding lecture mode creates a relational environment that helps her feel comfortable opening up to you more often. You'll even be able to throw in a thought or two of your own sometimes.

Top Ten Talking Tips

It's one of those golden moments. For some unknown reason, your daughter starts talking. Not only is she talking, she's sharing! Amazingly, words, sentences, and paragraphs flow from her. Appreciate these moments and facilitate more of them by minding these tips:

1. DON'T interrupt. When she's feeling chatty, she enters a flow. If you interrupt with a question or comment, the moment could vanish as quickly as it appeared. You don't have to be mute. Just be mindful of creating a lot of open space for her to keep talking.

> **DO** show attunement with your engaged body language. Offer her your full attention. DO throw in small questions that help her talk more about the topic. Most of her benefit comes from the actual talking (not from hearing your thoughts), so help her ventilate her feelings by supporting her to talk more.

> **DO** a quick scan of your muscle tension. If you're holding tension in your body, you're more likely to pounce into her conversation flow. If she's talking about something that provokes you, be especially vigilant to control your own emotions! Good listening correlates with a relaxed body, smooth breathing, and physical openness.

2. DON'T look too interested. If you look too interested, you may trigger an intrusion response, and she may feel the need to pull back. Break eye contact from time to time so as not to accidentally cross that invisible line from interest to intrusion. This can be confusing, because if you have two or more daughters, their invisible lines will have different locations. One daughter might share quite freely, while the other has an easily triggered intrusion alarm. Even more confusing, the same daughter may snap shut one day, while on another day, she will tolerate and indulge several of your questions.

> **DO** keep an interested yet relaxed facial expression. The balance between being interested yet not intrusive can be a delicate one. If you are a busy parent with little time to talk with your teen, she is likely hungry for more connection. If you work a lot, have many demands on your time, or are by nature or nurture more emotionally private, you may need to ramp up your interest.

> **DO** tread carefully and watch your daughter for signals as to how you're doing. Most teen girls have no problem letting you know when to back off.

3. DON'T indulge in a teaching moment. It's hard, but really—don't. People teach your daughter something every minute of the day. She's saturated! If she grumbles about something she feels stressed about, resist the impulse to problem solve. Just nod empathically. Any unsolicited suggestion you give will likely annoy her.

> **DO** express confidence in her ability to figure out whatever she needs: "I bet you'll handle this just right."

> **DO** ask her gently if she'd like your perspective or ideas. (Think butterfly, not bulldog.) If she says no, let it go.

> **DO** try to set up "learning moments." If your daughter plays volleyball, have her show you how to bump. If she loves art, ask her questions that allow her to expand your world of knowledge. If she's into anime, ask her to show you the characters and explain them to you. Becoming her student gives her a break from absorbing and an opportunity to bring you more fully into her world.

4. DON'T involve her friends. When groups of girls collect at one house or in a carpool, the personal conversations run like rivers. Sometimes other girls will give you information about your daughter or involve you in the lively talk while your daughter winces uncomfortably. (It's a cruel yet ultimately fortunate reality that teen girls will often share intimate details with other moms once removed from their own mom.) It's tempting to be opportunistic and engage the friends for more than you would get from your daughter.

> **DO** feel complimented by their demonstration of trust and ease if they share with each other when you're around.

> **DO** maintain a respectful boundary instead of becoming "one of the girls."

> **DO** resist this temptation, or your daughter will be mad at her friends—"I can't BELIEVE you let my mom know that about me!"—and you.

5. DON'T overidentify with her. If you've ever considered your daughter your "mini-me," ditch that thought forever. If you switch her focus to tell her how much she's like you, she may feel uncomfortable and back off her sharing. Teen girls are working on separating, and although parental intentions are well meaning, it is developmentally appropriate for teens to squirm away from intimate identifications with parents.

> **DO** keep a gentle focus on her. Listen to what she's saying and how she's feeling. Respect and remember that she is a completely separate person from you.

> **DO** shift from listening with your head to listening with your heart.

> **DO** remember COAL (curious, open, accepting, and loving).

6. DON'T show more emotion about what she's sharing than she does. If you get triggered into an intense reaction or express too much curiosity, fascination, or concern, she will feel as if she's blown it by sharing and shut down. Teen girls want to talk to adults but often resist because they don't want to worry them, feel judged, or be sanctioned with their freedom.

> **DO** let her know that you "feel" her and want to support her, even when the content of her conversation is troubling. Make sure *her* emotional experience is the centerpiece of the conversation.

> **DO** let her know you will check in with her later: "Honey, I'm glad you shared this with me. We can let it settle, and you can let me know what I can do to support you. We can generate some ideas together."

7. DON'T discuss her personal information with other people. Even if you're sharing neutral things about her, many teen girls feel violated and ashamed when their parents talk about them with other adults. Now she feels more like an adult and has a need for privacy. She may feel outraged when she hears you sharing information about her with your sister or friend. Sadly some girls don't give their parents a second chance after confidentiality has been breached.

> **DO** visualize putting the information on a very high shelf that you can't access without a ladder.

8. DON'T minimize the importance of what she says, even if you think it's just drama. Instead of judging the content, note aspects of her sharing that seem important to her.

> **DO** pay attention to the details and try to remember them. When the topic comes up again, your memory of the details translates to her as strong evidence of your love and her significance.

> **DO** avoid pinning a "happy face" on what she's saying (for example, saying, "This too shall pass," "Everyone has felt this way," "It could be worse"). She may feel insulted and trivialized. Instead say things like "Yeah, I get it" or "That must have felt really awkward."

> **DO** try to use some of the same language she has used. For example, when she's describing something as awkward, use similar language and resist interjecting a word like "humiliating," which does not fit what she's trying to convey.

9. DON'T jump on the bandwagon. If she's sharing an issue she's struggling with that concerns a relationship or some other challenge, resist the urge to also criticize or critique that person or situation: "Yeah, I always thought she was kind of flakey." When you jump on the bandwagon, she may backpedal or abandon her own exploration in order to manage your perception. She will worry that her venting may create a permanent judgment in your mind that will adversely affect her. It feels less safe to explore what's difficult or painful when you jump in too.

> **DO** concentrate on being present for her exploration. Try saying things like "What was that like for you?," "Sounds like a really hard situation," or "What do you hope will happen?" If the issue gets better for her, allow it to get better for you too. Don't get stuck on a bandwagon she's long forgotten.

10. DON'T jump to conclusions or project negativity. Teens often complain that they try to share with their parents, but the conversation veers out of control. It starts under the control of the teen but ends in the control of the parent. One teen complains that if she tells her mom about a cute boy at school, her mom takes over the conversation with too many questions, including questions about the boy's character and substance use, which makes the daughter feel offended and disrespected. The daughter responds to this by vowing to resist urges to share with her mom in the future. She feels hurt and angry that her mom gives her little credit for being a good decision maker.

DO project optimism and confidence whenever possible. Even if your daughter seems to be confused or making poor choices, let her know you believe in her ability to find a solution or make things better.

Teens Talk

Here's what teen girls say about what works for them when talking to adults:

o Even though I act bitchy, I really want my mom to be there for me. I want to talk but don't know what to say. I'm so relieved when my mom is patient with me and helps me start talking or just acts nice even though I don't really deserve it.

o I like when adults remember things about me. It makes me feel like they care enough to go beyond the basic "How's school?" conversation.

o I HATE being talked to in the morning, when my dad is most talkative. We worked it out after many bad mornings of him feeling like I was disrespectful. He even called me depressed, but really, I just hate mornings! Maybe parents should figure out what their daughter likes and keep it in mind.

o I like it when adults make it easy to talk to them—as opposed to them telling me how tall I am and going on and on about how grown up I've become. I mean, what am I supposed to say to that? Awkward!

The bottom line is that teen girls respond to an open, friendly style. If you can step out of your own feelings of social inadequacy or wariness with teens and tap into openness and warmth, they will see you as someone safe to talk to. If an amazing exchange does not ensue, know that you still made an impact that might feed into the next interaction, or the one after that.

More Tips for Even the Toughest Talks

Talking with teen girls can be challenging at the best of times. The challenge is even greater when you have to deal with a tough topic. Here are a few tips:

Consider timing. Especially when approaching your daughter about a touchy topic, give yourself time. Instead of moving too quickly and emotionally into conversation, set your internal dial to COAL: curious, open, accepting, and loving. Give your daughter time as well. Let her know you'd like to talk with her and offer her a few minutes or more to wrap up whatever she's doing: "Hey honey, I need you to shut down your computer and come talk with me for a while."

Consider location. Ask your daughter where she'd like to meet, or choose a room that's private and comfortable: "We can go into my room, or you can suggest another spot that you'd prefer."

Begin well. Put her at ease and serve as an example of how to take a positive approach to difficult conversations: "Some things are hard to talk about but still can't be avoided. I want us to have a productive conversation. I don't have an agenda to bust you or punish you. I just want to talk to you and also hear your thoughts and viewpoint. My bottom line is that I love you, even if we don't agree or I have a problem with your choices."

Consider wording. While managing the volume and tone of your voice, choose wording designed to minimize your daughter's defensiveness. In many instances, neutrally describing the concern serves as a solid beginning to your tough talk. For example, "Collette's mom called and said there was drinking at their house last night."

The power of noticing. In other instances, using the words "I've noticed…" can help you articulate a touchy topic without sounding accusatory or judgmental. For example, "I've noticed a change in your eating patterns" or "I noticed you seemed drunk (or high) when you came home last night."

Hand the conversation over. As soon as you've made your brief comment, hand the conversation over to her by inviting her to offer more information. For example, "What are your thoughts on this?" or "I'd like to hear from you what happened."

Remember calm listening. Listen to your daughter without escalating your emotional intensity. If she becomes defensive or angry, remind her that you are on her side, not against her. Remind her that you care about her. If she shares information that is disturbing, let her know that you appreciate her openness and that you will sit with the information. You may need to get support from other people or do some research to decide if more action is necessary.

Ask more useful questions. As you offer support, ask how she's feeling about the situation, how you can support her, and how she might handle the situation next time.

> Your commitment to caring more about her than her absolute honesty finds its mark even in the absence of complete disclosure.

Don't hold out for ultimate truth. When questions and answers lead to smooth conversations, your daughter may share helpful and accurate information. At the same time, she may share a partial truth or a complete lie. Teens cannot always be honest with their parents, and it's usually fruitless to focus on extracting ultimate honesty. This dishonesty does not mean she's on the road to becoming a pathological liar. Your commitment to caring more about her than her absolute honesty finds its mark even in the absence of complete disclosure.

Consider a twenty-four-hour "hold." If you "catch" your daughter in the act of a bad choice or misbehavior, you can stack the deck for a productive conversation by putting it on a twenty-four-hour hold. Tell her you'd like to talk about the situation in twenty-four hours so that she can have time to settle, get "off the spot," and be as honest as possible.

You now have the inside track on communicating with not only your teen but also teens in general. Talking with teens is often a surprisingly delightful and enlightening experience. They have a lot to say when they feel comfortable! Your new skills will also come in handy as you address ways to support your daughter's optimal health.

5

Eat, Sleep, Move:
Supporting Your Daughter's Health

Your daughter's body, from her brain to her feet, is experiencing huge changes. Some of these changes feel wonderful to teen girls and others feel downright traumatic. An unexpected weight spurt, for example, while very natural and common, can make a teen girl uncomfortable in her body. Problems with sleep are common. Teen girls get a second wind right about the time they need to be heading to bed. Fitting exercise into a busy schedule is an additional hurdle for teen girls and parents alike. With skillful guidance, you can help your daughter manage these and other challenges to create and sustain optimal health.

You May Be Noticing:

○ Your daughter cares more about appearance than health. She'll spend an hour on her hair but forget to eat breakfast.

○ She's exhausted yet lobbies passionately for a late night out. The two issues are unrelated in her mind.

○ She's critical about her size and weight. Either she doesn't seem to connect food choices and exercise with feeling good and confident in her body, or she's overly focused on restricting food and exercising her body.

○ She complains of aches, pains, skin issues, headaches, feeling "gross." Her solutions involve quick fixes or products rather than committing to consistent practices that yield long-term results.

Connecting the Dots

Teen girls don't consistently connect the dots regarding how daily decision making impacts how they look, feel, and function. Hence, they don't see the problem in planning an overnight before a soccer tournament. If they have a symptom that bothers them—whether it's acne, a tight hamstring, food sensitivity, or headaches—they don't connect lack of improvement with their lack of compliance to a treatment protocol. Teen girls may lament feeling too fat, too thin, exhausted, or stressed, yet drop the ball on rest, hydration, exercise, healthy meals, and other solid self-care.

> Remember that your daughter's fragility in the face of criticism (real or perceived) is at an all-time high in her teen years.

Someday your daughter will make thoughtful choices that produce desirable outcomes, and she will avoid choices associated with unwanted outcomes. Your chronically tired girl may tweak her evening routine to get more sleep and feel better the next day. Your stressed-out girl may go out for a run or walk to mitigate anxiety during finals. Eventually teen girls do connect the dots. Until then, parental support is necessary. Your approach will determine how well your daughter accepts your support.

Protecting the Messenger and the Message

Have you tried to help your daughter with health and safety choices only to experience a "shoot the messenger" effect? Because of their developmental stage, teen girls are quick to perceive parental input as invalidating or critical. Their emotions trump their self-control when they feel picked on or one down, provoking retaliatory verbal responses. Especially during heated discussions, it's important to remember that your daughter's fragility in the face of criticism (real or perceived) is at an all-time high in her teen years. Your skill is crucial to keeping the messenger, and the message, alive.

THREE TIPS FOR MESSENGERS

Tip 1: Choose your comments carefully. If you comment on too many things too often, virtually none of your messages connect. Your daughter will develop a strong filter to keep you and your messages out. Take a moment before speaking to ask yourself this question: Is this issue significant enough to make a point about?

For example, I have unsuccessfully harassed both my daughters about cracking their knuckles. (What is it with the knuckle cracking? My teen clients do it too.) My comments were fruitless and extremely annoying to my daughters—who, when they felt like it, let go of the habit on their own. Observe yourself to see if you're commenting on too much too often. If you tend to be a worrier or feel irritable, hold back many of your comments so that the ones that really count get through.

Tip 2: Keep the communication short and sweet. Your daughter's "filter" is activated at a certain word count. Teen girls change the limit depending on mysterious variables beyond our parental understanding. If you keep your comments brief, you increase the chance of message acceptance. Choose a few sentences and articulate your thoughts with emotional neutrality and without judgment or disapproval.

Tip 3: Choose teen-friendly wording. Phrases such as "You seem," "It seems like," "I wonder if," "I've noticed," or "I've heard (or read)" suggest a light and collaborative approach. Your daughter is much more likely to absorb your thoughts if you avoid presenting them as if you're the "expert." Expert mode is a huge turnoff to teen girls, and I avoid it both as a psychologist and as a mom. Respecting teen girls as equal, rather than "one down," allows them to stay open in the conversation and the relationship.

Putting the Tips into Action

The challenge, of course, is putting the tips into action in real-life situations. Here are examples of how to knit these tips together effectively:

On getting enough sleep. When you see your daughter dragging herself in the door after school, you could say, "Kayla, you seem really tired today, and I can see you're struggling. I wonder how many hours of sleep you got last night." Keep your voice warm and devoid of accusation. Sound rhetorical—as if you're wondering aloud but don't require an answer. Since your approach is compassionate and noncritical, your daughter can be open to what you've said and reflect on it herself.

On headaches and eating/drinking habits. You might say, "Sierra, I'm sorry your head hurts. I've noticed you seem to be drinking less water lately. And I found a lot of candy wrappers in the dryer. I wonder if there's a connection."

You're musing aloud about a possible connection but no answer is required, so your daughter doesn't feel confronted. Since she doesn't have to defend herself against a perceived criticism, she can contemplate the possible connection for herself.

You can also give her a tip without sounding like a know-it-all by saying something like this: "I've heard (or I've read) that dehydration often causes headaches."

On wearing a bike helmet. You might say, "Olivia, I noticed your helmet sitting on the porch while you were out on your bike. A bike accident can be very serious and even change your life forever. Keeping your head protected is vital to your safety." Then you may add, "I love you and your safety is really important. Please commit to wearing it no matter how short the distance."

Since the health risk in this example is serious, you can amplify its impact by sourcing an article about bike safety or bike accidents and pinning it to her door. Collateral reading allows you to bump up her awareness without being the sole messenger of the information.

CONNECTING THE POSITIVE DOTS

It's just as important—and sometimes even more important—to note positive connections for your daughter. By acknowledging favorable outcomes to her healthy choices and habits, you help her connect the dots regarding what she's doing right.

On improving eating, rest, and hydration. You might say, "Daisy, you brought so much energy and focus to the tournament today. It seems like your healthy eating and attention to sleep and hydration are serving you well."

On improving mood through exercise. You might say, "Cali, I can see how energized and content you feel when you get your swimming in."

Exercise: Helping Your Daughter Connect the Dots

Now it's time to consider how you can help your own daughter connect the dots—and how you can craft your comments in the most helpful way. Begin by listing three recurring health issues involving your daughter:

_____

_____

_____

Review the "Three Tips for Messengers" section above, and then write a few sentences that connect the dots for your daughter in the situations you listed above.

_____

_____

_____

Practicing new communication skills, a light hand, and a warm, supportive tone give you the power to positively influence your daughter's health and safety. A soft touch influences your daughter much more than a strong, controlling grip.

Good-Bye, Control—Hello, Influence

You've surely noticed, and perhaps lamented, that control over your daughter's choices decreases in the teen years. You can't keep her away from large amounts of sugar anymore, nor can you put her down for a much-needed nap. Alas, many of her choices, small and momentous, occur out of your jurisdiction.

You can still position yourself to be very influential. When you communicate in the collaborative manner you just practiced, your daughter feels less need to resist, reject, or rebel. She feels respected and loved. When you give up the need to control and instead embrace the power to influence, you cement a relationship with your daughter that keeps you both on the same side.

Not only will you get along better, but you will also diminish the intensity with which she pushes you away—and she'll carry your influence inside of her to guide her decisions. She won't unfailingly make choices that thrill you, but she'll make plenty of good choices.

Why Let Go of High Control?

If you are a *high-control* parent, it's time to modify your style, because high control tends to produce angry rebels. You can't always spot an angry rebel, because mild to serious symptoms can manifest themselves in subtle ways.

Highly controlled girls may comply with heavy-handed parenting for a while, but then develop problems when an internal flash point is activated. If highly controlled teen girls do not express their anger externally, they may bottle it up internally only to have it transform into depression or self-harming behaviors. To make matters more dangerous, highly controlled girls are loath to go to parents for help, support, or rescue when needed, because they fear disappointing their parents or being judged or rejected by them. Just as neglecting teen girls fails them, so does overcontrolling them.

> Let go of control; embrace influence.

What's the bottom line? Overcontrolled teen girls often turbo-launch into the very behaviors from which their parents try to protect them. Let go of control; embrace influence.

Exercise: Are You Too Controlling?

If you suspect you're too controlling—and even if you don't think you are—take a look at the statements below and check any that describe you:

_____ People tease you about being controlling or call you a control freak.

_____ You have lots of opinions you share *generously*.

_____ You feel like *losing it* when people disappoint you.

_____ You struggle with compromise.

_____ You have trouble listening without interrupting.

_____ You like your ideas the *very, very* best.

If you answered yes to one or more of these statements, it's time to shift gears. Lots of high controllers are wonderful, sweet, loving people, but you can't let yourself off the hook just because you're a sweet, loving controller! Love does not neutralize the harm caused by overcontrol.

If teen girls don't act out and instead toe the line for a controlling parent, they risk becoming approval junkies. Approval junkies have a tough road; they forgo authentic, multifaceted development in order to please others, which becomes their food for a starving self-esteem. Instead of being able to fund their own confidence and well-being, they depend on accolades and approval from others. Eventually such girls struggle with feelings of emptiness and resentment, having sacrificed themselves to meet the expectations of others on whom they are unhealthily dependent.

Your daughter deserves a better future than that. Sure, she can make people happy, but it should come as a byproduct of rich and authentic development—a development based on a deep connection with *her* thoughts, feelings, ideas, choices, and priorities. The teen years are crucial for all kinds of development, which can easily be thrown off course when girls get stuck capitulating to or rebelling against a controlling parent. It is against a teen girl's developmental blueprint to be controlled, so become an honest observer of your behavior and be willing to self-correct when you need to.

Exercise: What Can You Let Go?

Do you manage things for your daughter that she'd be better off managing for herself? You don't need to withdraw nurturing or supportive behaviors—just take a look at your behaviors to see if they fall on the side of care or control. To help you explore what you can let go, reflect on the questions below:

Has your daughter pushed back against any of your managing behaviors, or have you received outside comments on any of your managing behaviors? If so, which ones?

_____

_____

_____

Are there benefits associated with letting go of those behaviors? If so, what are they?

_____

_____

_____

Are there risks? If so, describe them.

_____

_____

_____

Discuss what you've written with your daughter to get her feedback. You might negotiate changes that work well for both of you.

Supporting Self-Sufficiency

To let go of overcontrol, focus more on yourself and less on your daughter. Notice how much time and effort you spend managing and directing her, and then pull back. Reposition yourself by asking *what outcome you seek*. Surely you don't want your daughter to resent and avoid you because you're too controlling. Teen girls often talk about feeling deeply offended by controlling parents because they feel their parents lack faith in them. While you might think, *I'm doing this out of love*, your daughter may think, *My mom and dad have absolutely no faith in me*. If you want your daughter to become increasingly self-sufficient while enjoying a positive connection with you, relax your controlling ways and practice feeling, believing, and expressing your confidence in her growing self-management.

You are metaphorically handing her the baton and cheering as you watch her move forward and figure out how to do such things as wake up in the morning, make appointments, and manage her schedule. Batons sometimes get dropped, and that's part of the learning process. When mistakes occur, reassure your daughter that people figure out how to get things right by sometimes getting things wrong. Replace heavy management with enjoying her; finding out what she needs, thinks, and wants; exposing her to interesting experiences and information; and delighting in who she is. Focus on positive time with her, sharing a laugh and reflecting her worth to her.

WELCOME THE PUSH-BACK

If you do make an unnecessary comment or catch yourself in overcontrol mode, allow your daughter to *push back* and sincerely consider her point: "Mom, I Googled knuckle cracking and it does *Not* cause arthritis or any serious problems." Support that plucky and developmentally appropriate behavior by throwing the fight and appreciating her intelligence, resourcefulness, and strength: "Duly noted, Marley. It's clearly my issue, and I won't say another word about it." Teen girls love it when parents admit they're wrong. It levels the playing field, which feels refreshing to them. It also models accountability, flexibility, and the willingness to value other people's feedback. Your teen girl feels important when you give up your point to embrace and respect hers.

Positive Influences: Exercise, Sleep, and Food

Now let's cover more ways to positively impact teen girls. During these years of rapid change, you can adopt practices and routines that will make a big difference in how your daughter feels about herself and her life. Learning healthy routines now enables her to take them with her into adulthood.

The Importance of Exercise

Teen years are a perfect time to participate in regular physical activity. Because teen girls undergo a systemwide growth spurt (weight as well as height), exercise quells a teen girl's sense of being out of control over her body. Teen girls regularly acknowledge reduced anxiety, improved mood, and improved ability to think well and concentrate as benefits of exercise. They also feel a sense of control and mastery over their lives that boosts confidence and self-esteem.

If your daughter develops a regular exercise habit, she'll feel more confident and comfortable as she moves through her world. In a culture that provides and markets junk food to teens constantly while simultaneously flooding them in superthin and super "sexy" female images, teen girls get little support to feel healthy, strong, and powerful in their radically changing bodies. Exercise as a means of caring for the body, as opposed to whipping it into shape, creates the right self-care orientation for teen girls.

Remember that, developmentally, teen girls are responding to an evolutionarily determined desire to look and be attractive. They want to feel loved, accepted, and good enough. It's not a

> Many teen girls work hard to be thin or sexy, not because they're looking for sex but because they're seeking to feel successful according to the standards of our culture.

superficial preoccupation; it's hardwired. In our super sexed-up culture, teen girls quickly note that the way to be attractive is to model themselves after the images they see in the media. Our consumer-driven society is happy to help by providing items such as padded, push-up bras for tweens! Many teen girls work hard to be thin or sexy, not because they're looking for sex but because they're seeking to feel successful according to the standards of our culture.

DREAM OR NIGHTMARE?

Be sensitive to the possibility that exercise is potentially a teen girl's worst nightmare. We all know it takes a lot to begin and sustain an exercise routine. Teen girls often avoid exercise because of self-consciousness and physical exhaustion. A tired teen girl struggling with feelings of awkwardness may not be stoked to accompany you to your gym for a step class. Encourage your daughter to be active without pushing too hard. Girls who feel bullied to exercise often get the wrong message: "My parents think I'm fat!"

Some teen girls overtrain their bodies in a panicked effort to control weight. Such behavior can signal an eating disorder, and such a teen will need loving help and patient support to transform self-punishment into self-love. Depending on how entrenched the distressed thinking and behavior become, professional help may be needed.

In the big picture, we want teens to incorporate reasonable and regular exercise into a healthy, balanced, and self-loving lifestyle. Regular exercise can help teen girls feel better emotionally as well as physically and can serve as a fabulous outlet for stress and big feelings. Socially, girls who participate in group activities or team sports can benefit from an expansion of personal relationships, which evolve along with all the goodies of being part of a team. Families that exercise together find they have fun, connect, and get a workout at the same time. Biking, hiking, swimming, backpacking, rock climbing, and going to the gym together promote both health and positive relationships.

If you like new experiences, start checking exercise-related events happening in your community. You may woo your daughter into doing a 5- or 10K race or walk to benefit charity. Training for a purpose can be a great way to get motivated. Knowing her participation benefits a good cause gives your daughter an opportunity to feel good and connect to humanity outside her immediate social relationships. Not all teen girls will be game for a 10K, however, so keep your eye out for other opportunities in your community. To increase the interest level, you might each ask a friend to join you. As exercise becomes part of their routine, girls see they can impact the way they feel, look, and perform through dedicated effort and commitment—nothing to sneeze at when so much in their lives feels beyond their control. Exercise often motivates teen girls to eat consciously too, a case of one good thing leading to another.

It's ideal for parents to help girls identify activities they like and, in a light and positive way, support them in connecting to those activities. Different girls will be candidates for different kinds of physical movement. One of my competition-averse clients found her bliss in belly-dancing class, while one of my overstimulated and restless clients cultivated a running program that helped her center and decompress. Here are some more suggestions:

Talk about exercise (and food) in terms of health, not in terms of weight. When people exercise and eat well, weight takes care of itself. Teen girls who learn to trust their bodies are less likely to fixate on overcontrolling food and exercise as a strategy to bully their size into place. Strong-arming the body with overcontrol only sets a teen girl up for a pendulum swing toward undercontrol, the hallmark of pernicious eating-disordered cycling. Even if your teen just has a big weight spurt, her body knows what to do to rebalance. The best thing she can do is to treat herself well every day—not to panic, not to rush, and not to push herself back toward a prepubescent body. You can be a major source of reassurance.

Be active yourself and create a win-win situation for you and your daughter. Take care of yourself, and you will teach your daughter through your example. Doesn't it make sense that active parents have active kids? If you exercise already, let your daughter see how well it works for you. She hears when you talk about how invigorated you feel after your walk, or how yoga makes you feel stronger, happier, and more focused.

Tune in to the activities that fit with your daughter's interests and her personality. If it's not her style to get out and dance in front of other people, she may be a better candidate for a Pilates DVD she can do in the privacy of her own home, or running on a home treadmill. If she's expressive and dramatic, she may enjoy a dance class that includes a performance opportunity. If she's stressed or has difficulty focusing, she may love the way yoga helps take stress down a notch while enhancing mental clarity. Generate ideas, but always see what she thinks.

Give your daughter the 411 about creating new habits, like exercising. It can be very hard to create a new habit. After three weeks or so, however, the new habit will kick in, and it will feel "weird" *not* to exercise! Also, it's much easier to *maintain* an exercise routine than to *begin* one. Similarly it's much easier to *stay* in shape than to *get* in shape. Your daughter can feel proud of herself every time she follows through with her commitment. Before long, her exercise plan will feel like part of who she is and how she lives her life.

Another great advantage to regular exercise is better sleep. Since teen girls typically experience a lot of changes in their sleep patterns, let's look at how you can help your daughter sleep better.

The Importance of Sleep

"But I'm not tired!" She's not kidding, she really isn't tired. It's 11 or 12 at night and your daughter is still the sharpest tool in your family shed. In 2002, sleep researcher Mary Carskadon described a change in the teenage brain affecting the circadian system. It turns out that the teen brain releases the sleepy chemical melatonin up to two hours later than adult or preteen brains. To make the situation harder, when a teen girl is supposed to be waking up ready to roll on a fresh day of learning, her brain is *still* releasing melatonin (Carskadon 2002). Just as intensity of learning is on the wax for teen girls, sleep is on the wane.

Sleep experts say that while many teens are able to survive on too little sleep, they actually need nine hours to function well. Mood, memory, growth, learning, test scores, and emotional control all take a serious hit when teens don't get enough sleep (Strauch 2004). The next time your daughter has a meltdown, forgets something important, or underperforms on a test, consider sleep deprivation to be a possible culprit.

To support teens, some schools are changing start times to a more brain-friendly hour. In fact, in 2002 Kyla Wahlstrom and her research team at the University of Minnesota reported that when a high school in Minnesota changed its start time from 7:25 to 8:30, math SAT scores of the brightest students bumped up 56 points and verbal SAT scores bumped up an astonishing 156 points! Those students also reported higher motivation and lower levels of depression (University of Minnesota 2002). Hopefully results like this will lead to later start times for high schools across America.

In 2011, I interviewed sleep specialist Dr. Aaron Morse of the Central Coast Sleep Center in Santa Cruz, California. Dr. Morse noted that sleep deprivation is correlated with a range of problems: mood instability; irritability; depression; elevated levels of the stress hormone cortisol; and an impaired ability to process glucose, which can contribute to obesity and type 2 diabetes. Dr. Morse also noted that difficulty with concentration is common and puts sleepy teens at high risk for drowsy driving and for accidents caused by falling asleep.

SLEEP TALK

Believe it or not, most teens are fascinated to hear about their changing brains. When you start a conversation about sleep with your daughter, start off by sharing that teen brains actually secrete melatonin later in the day, therefore causing the delay in sleepiness at night. Most teens appreciate the notion that their sleep resistance isn't entirely their fault. You can even commiserate with her: "No wonder you want to stay up so late!" It puts you on the same side.

Then let her know there is other interesting research about teens and sleep. Share a few sound bites from the information cited above, or research some of your own, so that she can understand what motivates your interest in proper sleep: "I don't want to make your life miserable by hounding you about sleep, but I want you to know how important it is to your learning, memory, mood, and almost everything. I want you to manage it yourself, and I'll just be your backup support."

Are there other ways that you can encourage your daughter to get a good night's sleep? Here are a few suggestions:

Encourage her to turn off all media an hour or more before bedtime, in order to reduce her level of stimulation. Removing media from her room removes the temptation and downsizes the media habit.

Help her connect the dots with sleep-inducing activities she enjoys: a warm bath, pleasure reading, sleepy tea blends. Support her in avoiding high-energy activities in the evening and all forms of caffeine from noon on. Even chocolate contains enough caffeine to disrupt a teen girl's sleep.

Help her set a reasonable bedtime. Most parents don't do this, which means girls set their own. Instead of telling her a time, you can ask her, "Based on the research about nine hours being crucial, at what time do you think you need to begin your sleep routine?" Then you can support her ideas: "Okay, so we need to get dibs on the bathtub for you around 9 o'clock so you can start winding down."

The Importance of Food

Roused from insufficient sleep, what does a drowsy teen girl loathe more than springing into action at an early hour? Yep, the thought of looking at, smelling, and actually eating food. Help your daughter to understand that her body is a vehicle that transports her through her day. It requires energy (fresh, healthy food and plenty of water) to move, think, and feel well.

Here are some ways parents have integrated healthy eating into their family routines. Modify them or create others that will work for you and your daughter.

○ My daughter now makes a food list every weekend for the upcoming week. Sometimes she shops with me. When I presented the list idea, I let her know I really want to work with her and not nag her. I said that since I'm willing to shop with her ever-changing tastes in mind, she needs to be willing to do her part, which is to eat breakfast every day and work on making good nutrition choices.

○ I have my daughter ask her friends what they're enjoying, and we use it for inspiration. My daughter seems to really like surveying her friends for their latest food favorites. We keep a list of ideas on the fridge. Her friends know we like inspiration, so they take part by writing their latest good meal on the list. That's how we learned about miso soup for breakfast, which my daughter loves, and roasting a big pan of veggies to add to everything from eggs to salads all week long.

○ We try to keep breakfast fun by experimenting with new smoothie recipes. Protein powder and other supplements boost the nutritional value.

As far as lunch goes, bringing good healthy food from home stacks the deck for better nutrition. Your best bet is to work collaboratively with your daughter to try and stock foods she likes.

FAMILY DINNER

There are many compelling reasons to prioritize eating dinner as a family. Emotionally it gives family members a sense of connection and safety. It reminds busy teens that they are part of a special unit that shares life and love. Socially it promotes an opportunity for communication. With the texting they do all day, at dinner teens get a chance to practice real, live communication with parents, siblings, and guests. Some teens benefit from a gentle prompt: "Would anybody like to hear about my day? I have things to share." Some families tell about one experience from their day. Even a teen who's feeling uncommunicative will usually comply with that one.

Nutritionally, teens benefit from homemade dinners as opposed to food grabbed on the go. Family dinners often include fresh, unprocessed foods with more nutrition and less fat and sodium. Portion sizes are likely to be more moderate and food consumed more consciously when eating at a table. Financially most people find that making dinner at home is less expensive. One of the benefits of the nation's economic downturn has been a reclaiming of family dinnertime.

New information about the importance of family dinners is very encouraging. In his 2009 book *How to Raise a Drug-Free Kid*, Joseph A. Califano Jr. states that eating together five to seven times a week is associated with lower rates of teen smoking, drinking, and illegal drug use (Califano 2009). *Wow!*

Who would have guessed the effects of eating as a family could be so far-reaching? It's worth boosting your effort for benefits this numerous. But if you find it a challenge to have dinner together, go for progress, not perfection, by adding a family dinner to your week whenever you can.

DANGER ZONE: FOOD AND EATING DISORDERS

For some girls, efforts to control food and weight become agony. During their preteen and teen years, girls are very vulnerable to the development of eating disorders. Different factors put girls at risk. Perfectionist girls may start losing weight in order to attain our culture's view of physical perfection (thin with breasts). Compliments from others reinforce the unhealthy commitment. Formerly thin girls can feel so traumatized by adolescent weight gain that it opens the door for a compulsive and punishing "corrective" response. Girls known for their slimness can feel compelled to avoid increasing curviness, triggering a dangerous diet-gone-bad nightmare. Stressed or disempowered girls may overfocus on food restriction and exercise as a way of expressing anger or gaining a sense of control. Girls who feel oppressed by expectations (internal, parental, or cultural) and limited freedom may channel their frustration and pain into starving their bodies: a mix of bingeing and starving, or bingeing and purging. Eating disorders are rampant and taking hold of girls earlier than ever before.

Because they can lead to severe health problems and even death, eating disorders are serious business and require expert support for parents and teen girls. If you notice changes in your daughter's eating habits, postmeal behavior, and/or weight, *approach her sensitively*. Because this topic inspires so much concern, parents may move toward their daughter with a lot of emotional intensity. Unfortunately that often increases the tenacity of the eating disorder. Instead of extinguishing the problem, it is driven farther underground, and the teen girl may go to greater lengths to hide it.

Eating-distressed girls need support and patience. Parents of eating-distressed girls need support too. Take care of yourself so you can collaborate with your daughter against the problem. It's you and your daughter against a health risk, not you against your daughter. Put a support team together that includes a nutrition specialist, a family doctor knowledgeable about the treatment of eating disorders, and an experienced therapist.

I'd like to close this chapter with two important points. First, to be safe, never, ever comment on anyone's weight, not even to compliment. Compliments can trigger obsession just as criticism can. If you want to pay a compliment, tell someone she looks radiant, lovely, energized, or happy. Second, never speak critically of your own body—especially if you're a mom. If you're working on getting into shape, phrase your communication carefully so you model the right attitude for your daughter. Love yourself into shape; don't hate yourself into shape. Your healthy, self-loving approach to your body serves as a powerful example to your daughter.

Now that we've covered essential health matters, let's move on to see how we can support our girls in making safe choices in other areas of their lives.

6

Walking on the Wild Side: Supporting Safe Decision Making

Risky behavior has been around since we were teenagers and long before. While certain fads in risk taking come and go, the foundational trio of temptations remains sex, drugs, and alcohol. Throw driving in with any of the three and you get even more risk and higher parental anxiety.

There are solid reasons teen girls are pulled to walk on the wild side. They want adventure, independence, and a sense of belonging. Even their brain development creates a pull toward experimentation, pleasure seeking, and novel experiences. At the same time, since the teen brain is still a work in progress, safe decision making is hindered by an inability to consistently or reliably anticipate and plan for consequences. Such operations are under the purview of the prefrontal cortex, the last part of the teen brain to develop!

You May Be Noticing:

○ Your daughter displays more "sexiness" than you'd like. And if she doesn't, she watches sexualized shows / movies / music videos, reads sexy books, and listens to sexualized lyrics. You'd like to touch base with her about the topic of sexuality but fear that "death penalty" facial expression you're sure to get.

○ You wonder if she's using substances. You give dual-purpose hugs: to give some love, of course, but also to sneak in a surreptitious smell check.

○ You worry about her behavior beyond your supervision. She's so private, and your inquiries so poorly received.

Teen Experimentation with Sex, Drugs, and Alcohol

The challenge of these teen years is that our daughters face the pressures of the risk-taking trio *well before* they've established the ability to make clear decisions and set reasonable boundaries. Pressure doesn't imply that others are standing next to our teens actively cajoling them to take part in risky behavior. Pressure refers to the unrelenting marinade of messages coming from the culture. These messages lace together with incomplete brain development and flourishing sexual development to create a seduction into behaviors such as drinking, smoking pot, and "hooking up." Even very young girls absorb cultural messages, which is why you see little girls dressing like they're twenty-one, displaying a pseudosophistication that's disconcerting for their age.

If you talk to your teen about cultural pressure, there's a good chance she won't nod and contribute greatly to a conversation. Teen girls feel that the choice to either engage or abstain is theirs, and they are offended if you suggest a wider sphere of influence. They don't identify our cultural value system, as promoted through the media, as a backdrop of pressure. It's simply the world they've grown up in. Their viewing and their music is everyday entertainment, and they have no reason to question its impact. Still, they are conditioned by the messages. We're all affected by cultural messages that consciously and unconsciously affect our values, choices, and priorities. Teen girls, however, are especially vulnerable to being adversely affected by them.

In time, teen girls cultivate a sense of personal boundaries and values. For some, experimentation is part of their value- and boundary-refinement process. Decisions, good and otherwise, offer information and experience that help girls get clear on what's okay for them and what's not. Some girls use therapy to process how they feel about their experimentation, since a therapist can facilitate examination without the emotional charge of a parent. If adults can be nonjudgmental toward an experimenting teen, conversation can facilitate reflection while increasing knowledge. No matter where a teen girl is on the experimenting continuum, having a strong relationship with at least one parent is a point of resilience.

For other girls, experimentation is minimal because they already feel clear about their values, are low-risk takers, or fear the lowering of an authoritative hammer. Some will experiment once they get to college, while others will never feel the need to experiment much at all. While certain parents become absolutely devastated when their teen daughter experiments, I have learned not to jump to conclusions about what such behavior ultimately creates or means. I have seen many girls who used their experimentation experiences to ultimately put together a very solid and safe code of conduct and values.

What's the bottom line? Most girls will gradually develop clear decision-making skills and become confident articulating reasonable boundaries. Until they do, they need guidance, support, and protection.

Different Parental Reactions

Many parents wish they could adopt a guaranteed, one-size-fits-all approach to escorting teens safely through these years. Instead, there's a wide spectrum of approaches and parental styles. At one extreme are parents who articulate few boundaries and expectations around sex, drugs, and alcohol. Some allow drugs, alcohol, and parties in their homes, believing that this choice keeps teens safer than if they were to explore such activities outside the home. Some also allow sexual activities by not creating barriers and guidelines for such behavior.

At the other extreme are zero-tolerance parents. They state zero tolerance and expect zero experimentation, which produces either a zero experimenter or an experimenter who hides the behavior. Some experimenting teens are discreet and "succeed" at evading parental awareness, while others "get busted," precipitating a crisis in the parent-teen relationship. The more the teen experiments and the more extreme the behavior, the more likely it is that parents or others become aware of the behavior. In general, zero-tolerance parents express their expectations, depict risky behaviors as intolerable or unacceptable, and move on, unless or until they become aware of a violation in policy.

With the two extremes noted, a huge amount of parents bob around in the middle, struggling to give messages that are neither permissive nor rigid. Often such parents and their teens feel tangled in good intentions and confused by mixed messages. Here's how one teen described her experience:

> My mom and dad have always told me I can be honest with them no matter what. Last week my mom pushed me about whether my boyfriend and I were having sex. So I told her yes, and that I would actually like to get on the pill. Her face went completely white and she pulled back from me like I just pooped on the floor. I guess she wants me to be completely honest unless I tell her something she doesn't want to hear.

Being Clear about Your Expectations and Messages

Sometimes we have a tough time getting through shocking moments like the one above. This mom found there was a big difference between suspecting and knowing her daughter was sexually active.

Thank goodness, we don't need to be perfect parents when we face challenging situations. We just need to let our girls know we're doing our best and are willing to make adjustments along the way. In this case, the mom needed time to regroup, digest the information, and get clarity for herself regarding the messages she wanted to send to her daughter. She apologized to her daughter for her initial shock and made an appointment with a gynecologist known to provide education as well as excellent health care to teen girls. She encouraged her daughter to talk to both her and the doctor about questions and concerns. She provided her daughter with books and articles on topics related to teen sexuality.

Before you can be clear with your daughter, be clear with yourself.

This mom also initiated a heart-to-heart talk about the significance and risks (emotional and physical) involved in a sexual relationship. She chose to make a clear boundary regarding the family home being a no-sex zone. The daughter and boyfriend were welcome together in the house but shut doors and spending the night were not an option. As a result, the sexual part of this teen's relationship progressed more slowly, giving ample opportunity for elements such as good communication and nonsexual intimacy to flourish. Although the daughter was not thrilled by in-home restrictions and fought for the privacy of closed doors, she felt her mom worked really hard to consider her best interest and gave her credit for that. She also noted that slowing down the sexual trajectory of her relationship was good for her and the relationship.

Before you can be clear with your daughter, it helps to be clear with yourself. When girls are younger, we can put off thinking about how we're going to handle experimentation. When girls become teens, it's time to clarify both expectations and important messages to communicate to them. The following exercise will help you identify where you stand. If you share parenting, use this exercise to build a parenting philosophy together. Most parents are not in perfect alignment, which works out fine as long as overt sabotage of one another is avoided. Even parents with different opinions on sex and drug use can share the value of prioritizing a solid relationship with their daughter *over* whatever challenge they face.

Exercise: Parenting Then and Now

Some parents tend to parent the way they were parented. Others make a concerted effort to do things differently and, hopefully, better. Think about how you were parented and answer these questions:

Were your parents strict/lenient/in-between? Describe:

_____

_____

_____

Did their approach work for you? Explain:

_____

_____

_____

What would you like to change, or keep the same, in raising your teen girl?

_____

_____

_____

To Share or Not to Share Your Experiences

Many parents wonder how much about their own experimentation history they should share with teen daughters. While there is no single answer appropriate for everyone, there are considerations to factor into your own choice.

For example, does your daughter *ask* about your history? If she doesn't inquire, you don't need to get into it unless you feel she would benefit from knowing some part of your history. If she does inquire, what is she hoping to get from knowing more? Ask her and you will likely learn something that will help you move forward in your decision. If she gives you a devilish grin, she may just want to "have something on you." Alternately she may want to feel a connection with you and learn from experiences you've had. If so, you may want to share.

If you do share, however, do not share anything that is still traumatic for you. Nor should you lapse into a reverie of "the good old days," which romanticizes your wild times. You need to have a sense of emotional mastery over the material. If you're still upset by an experience, don't transfer that traumatic energy to her. Get clear about the "takeaway" message you want your daughter to receive. If you can't identify a benefit, don't share. If it doesn't feel right in your gut to share, honor that instinct.

Exercise: Comfort Zone

To help you determine whether or not to share your experiences, write yes or no in response to each statement.

_____ My daughter expresses interest about my teen experimentation.

_____ I feel her curiosity is genuine and nonmanipulative.

_____ I have some experiences I think she could benefit from knowing about.

_____ I'm comfortable sharing these experiences with my daughter.

_____ I'm sure I could share in a way that would be useful and also positive for our relationship.

_____ I'm sure I could share with emotional stability, which protects my daughter from taking on any of my unresolved feelings associated with the experiences I'm choosing to share.

Yes answers may support your choice to share. If you answered yes to any or all of these questions, what would you like to share?

_____

_____

_____

How would you like your daughter to benefit from the conversation?

_____

_____

_____

Be Clear about Expectations

To clarify your own expectations about your daughter's behavior, it may be helpful to look at those commonly held by other parents. Note how you feel about each one.

- I expect my daughter to stay away from drugs and alcohol while she's living in my home.

- I expect my daughter to use sense in experimentation and not go overboard.

- I expect my daughter to be honest when I ask her about drugs and alcohol.

- I expect my daughter will partake in behavior that she hides or lies about.

- I expect my daughter to save sex for marriage or for after high school.

- I expect my daughter may become sexual as a teenager.

Use the above statements to clarify your own attitudes. One parent wrote the following:

Although I would prefer no experimentation, I did as a kid and I expect there's a good chance my daughter will too. I expect it would be hard for her to be honest but, if approached, that we could possibly talk about what she's doing, especially if it became concerning. I expect my daughter might become sexual in the context of a close relationship. I would want to share some of my thoughts about sex with her, most importantly that it is a significant decision and I want her to consider it carefully. I'd like to share aspects to consider such as sexual health and also the emotional vulnerability that comes with a sexual relationship.

Exercise: My Expectations

Write a few sentences below that summarize your thoughts and expectations regarding sex, drugs, and alcohol. Include whatever you feel strongly about.

_____

_____

_____

Be Clear about Messages

When dealing with experimentation, we need to be clear about the messages that we send to our daughters. Read what other parents have to say about messages they want to send:

- I want my daughter to know I'll be there for her in any emergency or bad situation, even if she's up to something I wouldn't approve of.

- I want my daughter to know it's never okay to drive under the influence of a substance or to allow someone under the influence to drive.

- I want my daughter to practice safe sex if she's sexual, and come to me for support.

- I want my daughter to know I will always love her, even if I don't like her choices.

- I want my daughter to regard sex as special and something to share with someone she really loves and trusts.

- I want my daughter to know that the less she puts drugs and alcohol into her growing brain and body, the better.

Another parent wrote:

I've definitely given the message about wanting my daughter to call me in any bad situation or emergency. Even though she rolls her eyes, I know she hears me and trusts that I mean it. I've told her that she needs to wait before drinking alcohol because it's dangerous for her brain and safety, and it's also illegal. If she does drink, she needs to think about what kind of setting she's in and how much she's going to put into her body. I don't want her to be one of those girls who has sex for the first time because she's under the influence. I need to tell her that. All of this makes me anxious, but I want to give clear messages.

Sometimes we parents have an expectation or a message that we forget to articulate! We assume our kids know, even though we haven't explicitly told them. Review your list of expectations and messages, and make sure you've actually communicated them to your daughter.

Village Support: Enlisting the Help of Others

Teens often resist going to their parents for support. Having a "village" not only benefits little kids, it also benefits teenagers. Are there trusted adults in your daughter's life she can turn to? Do you have close relatives or family friends who are willing to befriend your daughter? If so, ask them to tell your daughter that they are available to support her. Let your daughter know you fully support her talking to trusted family and friends, and, if it is not a life-or-death issue, their conversations can remain confidential. Convey your bottom line: You want her to feel supported and to have safe, caring people to confide in. You understand and accept she may not always feel comfortable talking to you.

Exercise: Listing Resource People

Think about three people you trust to whom your daughter could go to for support. Discuss them with your daughter, and then ask if they are willing to offer their support to your daughter. Make a list of these people—include name, address, phone, cell phone, and e-mail—and give your daughter a copy. Some parents include the list in their family phone book.

When offered a list of resource people, one teen girl said:

When my dad gave me contact information for three of our close family friends, I felt embarrassed and told him it wasn't necessary. But he insisted and really sounded like he wanted me to have more than just him to talk to. I didn't contact anyone for a year and I really thought I never would, but then I had a dilemma that I didn't want to talk to him about. I e-mailed one of my support people and we set up a coffee date to talk. I was nervous, but this person has known me since I was little and made me feel really comfortable. She helped me think through my dilemma without freaking out, and I felt really supported. My dad was looking out for me!

Matching Freedoms to Development

Teen girls respond best to parents who are neither rigid nor permissive. Such parents have expectations, rules, and guidelines, yet they also work with their daughters to revise unrealistic expectations, make occasional or appropriate exceptions, and expand freedoms as girls become older and more responsible. Effective parents learn to graduate freedoms reasonably and appropriately considering their daughter's age and maturity.

We all experience stressful moments when our daughters present requests, often communicated with great passion and urgency, that we haven't previously contemplated. For example, how do you feel about teen girls attending parties where alcohol is present? How do you feel about teen girls going to concerts without a parent along? How do you feel about your teen driving around on weekend evenings? How do you feel about her going

> Teen girls respond best to parents who are neither rigid nor permissive.

89

out without a precise plan? (Teen girls get really tired of being required to have a precise plan.)

Parents who are neither rigid nor permissive tend to engage their daughters in thoughtful conversations geared toward analyzing different aspects of such requests. Girls benefit from learning to modulate their feelings in these discussions as they present relevant information. They also benefit from parental ability to serve as auxiliary troubleshooters and planners, since teens don't always consider potential risks or challenges when they make their plans. In general, as teen girls evolve, so can their freedoms.

Let your daughter know again and again that presenting her plan to you, with relevant information, is part of the process of accessing freedom. Teen girls want what they want, which makes plan presentation challenging. It takes a lot for them to regulate their intensity and present needed information without losing their cool, so be patient and feel great about helping your daughter exercise her ability to tolerate strong emotions while negotiating effectively. We adults use that skill in our everyday lives, so we know how important it is to master!

Younger Teen Girls

To match freedoms and boundaries to the level of development, parents start with a sense of how mature their teen is for her age. In general, younger teens are less mature and have less life experience and judgment. You can offer opportunities for independent experiences incrementally and assess how well your teen is able to navigate each one. Freedoms can increase as your teen demonstrates her ability to handle them. You both learn as you go along.

> Identify yourself as a collaborator by letting her know that you are excited for her to have more freedom and want to work with her.

Connect the dots with your teen so she can see that her successes create more opportunities for independence. When she remembers to do her phone check-in, or to physically be at the appointed pickup location, let her know this responsible behavior gives you more and more confidence in her ability to handle further freedoms.

Whenever possible, reflect your daughter's successes to her. Good begets more good: "Thanks for sticking with our plan exactly, Dani. It gives me confidence to say yes the next time," or "Your teen years are going to be fun! Your level of responsibility with new privileges gives me a lot of confidence that you're ready for them." The positive connection you've developed with your daughter serves as a loving anchor during this time of increasing independence.

CREATING A FREEDOM WISH LIST FOR YOUNG TEENS

It's very helpful for parents and young teens to discuss potential freedoms. Use the following exercise as a way to initiate discussion.

Exercise: Increasing Freedom—Making a Wish List

Sit down with your teen daughter, in her early teens if possible, and make a list of freedoms she would like to pursue. She may need you to help her generate ideas. Getting dropped off with a friend to see a movie, going out to breakfast without an adult, going to study at a coffee house with a friend, or independent trips around the neighborhood are examples of forays young teens appreciate.

If your daughter is full of ideas, help her put them in an order of what can come first and what needs to come later. Identify yourself as a collaborator by letting her know you are excited for her to have more freedom and want to work with her. When she sees your goodwill toward her increasing independence, as opposed to picking up on your fear and resistance, she's likely to be a better sport when some of her requests meet the inevitable *no*. She will feel that you can accept that she is growing up.

If she doesn't feel you accept her developing independence, she may extend her boundaries secretly. Your confidence and goodwill toward her growing independence infuses her with optimism that you believe she can do well with independence. If and when mistakes are made or problems occur, rather than giving her the idea she's back to square one, collaborate with your daughter to harvest valuable learning from the experience.

THE LIST TELLS YOU A LOT

You can tell something about your teen by the freedoms she includes on her wish list. You may have a "think big, go big" teen girl with a big spirit and a big appetite for life and independence. Take a deep breath and accept that this type of teen presents joys as well as challenges. A good message for your high-risk taker would be "I love your passion for life! We'll work together to balance your independence with a reasonable step-by-step progression, okay?" But because she thinks big, you will find yourself needing to say no more often, which isn't fun for either of you. Reassure her by making it very clear that her growing independence and freedom is a step-by-step process. She will hear yes more as she shows she can handle smaller freedoms—and as she gets older!

You may have a low-risk taker who has trouble identifying freedoms she wants to pursue. No problem! Let her take her time and find her own comfort level. Some girls need to stay in the nest a good long while before taking a solo flight. As your daughter matures, you can both start noticing more purposefully small freedoms that might suit her.

YOUR ROLE AS A TRANSITIONAL BOUNDARY

Younger teens have a hard time saying no for fear of disappointing friends or others. Saying no is a way of asserting a boundary and choosing what you want or need. Since belonging and feeling accepted means everything to young teens, saying no is stressful because it stirs fears of rejection. While your daughter may be able to say no to you just fine, it's natural for her to struggle setting that boundary with other people in her life.

Until young teens develop the strength and clarity to set boundaries themselves, they benefit from parental willingness to serve as a "transitional" boundary. For example, your young teen daughter is asked to loan her brand-new shoes to her friend. She doesn't know how to answer. She wants to say no but feels shaky about it. Here's where you come in: you can be her excuse, her transitional boundary. She'll end up saying something like this: "Uh, I wish I could loan you those shoes, but my parents won't let me loan clothes." Let her know she can always use you as the reason to say no—you always have her back.

DUE DILIGENCE

With younger teens, you'll have many opportunities to practice due diligence. This includes touching base with parents who supervise parties, activities, or sleepovers. As you develop relationships with key social connections in your daughter's life, you have opportunities to establish mutual trust with fellow parents with whom you can collaborate in developing clear boundaries. Due diligence also includes saying no to a plan with associated risks that overwhelms your daughter's stage of development. For example, "Sorry, Hannah. You're too young to take a bus with your friends to the city and hang out all day. That's something you can do when you're older. We're building up to freedoms like that." This is a much better option than "Are you crazy, Hannah? No way are you going to the city with all those whack jobs and lowlifes!"

Older Teen Girls

As your daughter gets older, you'll sense her ability to make good decisions. Hopefully you will see her manage responsibilities better and better. She'll seem more adult and comfortable handling a range of interactions in the world. It's likely that her appetite for freedom will increase as she becomes more secure and confident. As her freedoms increase, match your conversations to the risks associated with the freedoms.

Too often parents convey excessive worry to their teen daughter. Excessive worrying about safety produces anxiety and insecurity in teen girls, not protection! Parents may feel their worry comes from love, but it translates as mistrust of the world and mistrust of the teen to navigate in the world. Or it produces *parental shutout,* a reflexive strategy activated in some teen girls who perceive parents to be over-the-top protective. Parental shutout involves the teen going "rogue" to pursue activities outside parental awareness. The teen perceives the parent as so stifling and protective that she must make a full mental split from the parent in order to pursue the freedom she desires. Paradoxically, if that fearful parent were more moderate, the teen would consider some of the parental input more fully and possibly be safer overall.

There are more benefits when parents convey good faith in the world and in their teen. Let her know her life management skills show you that she can handle freedom.

Discuss potential risks in a calm, informational manner without overblowing the fear factor. Breathe, and enjoy your daughter's growing independence. There's something about watching your teen daughter drive away from home that inspires powerful feelings of pride, joy, excitement, poignancy, and heartache.

If you have a daughter who navigates her life quite well—managing school, chores, self-care, and more—say yes a lot! Often parents don't let go of heavy management of their teen even when there's every indication they can. There's a good chance your daughter will soon be living independently, so if all systems appear to be go, allow her plenty of room to make the most of her own decisions.

PRACTICE SAYING NO

Whenever possible, we want to coach our daughters in how to say no. Socialized to be pleasing, even strong girls can have trouble saying no. Girls need to be supported in trusting their gut about a situation instead of responding in a way that keeps everyone happy. You can even supply information to her in anecdote form: "You know, if I'm in a movie theater and someone sits next to me who gives me an uncomfortable feeling, I just get up and move without feeling the least bit embarrassed or apologetic. I want you to do the same. Don't worry about hurting people's feelings!" Or, "If you're out and about and get a creepy feeling from someone, trust your gut and act on the feeling by getting yourself safe." Discussing and practicing different ways to increase safety can follow, such as leaving an unsafe environment, entering a store, yelling for help, getting around more people, asking a safe person (such as a mother with children) for assistance, requesting an escort to her car at night, making a phone call for support, and so on. Since teen girls are extremely embarrassed to make a big deal about feeling "creeped out," reading books or taking workshops about personal safety can help them become more confident. We can fully support them to do whatever they need to do to keep safe whenever their intuition warns them they are not.

> Girls need to be supported in trusting their gut about a situation instead of responding in a way that keeps everyone happy.

Generally, later in teen years, girls have developed the ability to advocate for themselves. They have had many opportunities to demonstrate how well they've handled previous freedoms, collaborated on plans, and respected family rules. Of course, many girls—older and younger—hit some bumps along this path.

Going over the Bumps

If your daughter hits a bump (or several) as she navigates a more precarious path, preserve your positive relationship with her. Parents who come down extremely hard on a teen girl who's blown it often leave the teen feeling traumatized and alienated. To deal with the sense of emotional extradition, she may adopt an "I really don't care" attitude. More dangerously, she may experience a sense of deep shame or anger that transmutes into accelerated risky behavior.

Parental comments such as "I don't know who you are anymore," "I'm so disappointed in you," "How could you do this to me?," or "How can I ever trust you again?" have the power to strip a teen girl down too far. They create an experience of shame and completely fail to promote learning or reflection. Because teen girls are so eager to please and to feel lovable and acceptable, no matter how aloof they seem, avoid reactions that strip, shame, and alienate.

So what's the bottom line? Coming home drunk, sneaking a boy in after hours, lying about where she is, and other "blow its" are still ideal times to connect the dots with teen girls. Wait until things settle, and instead of lowering the hammer, approach your daughter to explore the behavior. If you're more curious and interested than ragingly angry, she'll allow you access to her thoughts and feelings and even allow you to add a few thoughts she hasn't considered. For example, "We need to talk about you coming home drunk last night. I'm concerned about your choice to drink and whatever other choices you made in that state. But more than anything, I want to you to know that I love you and I want to support you with what's going on in your life lately."

These conversations with teen girls can be very bonding. When met with loving concern, teen girls are often touched and relieved that they let parents in. The teen girl must perceive that her parents care more about her than the behavior, so parental self-control must be very carefully managed: "I can see why you'd have trouble talking about this because you're a great kid and a great person, and you don't like the feeling you're in trouble. Punishing you is not my goal. Supporting you and helping you figure things out is!" Or, "You know honey, just because we're having this discussion doesn't mean I'm going to lose respect for you or forget who you are apart from this incident. I know how to keep perspective. We can talk about this without you feeling everything good about you, or our relationship, has been crushed. I know how to hold the big picture, even when the little picture is upsetting."

Sometimes you need to fake it till you make it as a parent. You may not actually feel as calm as you are presenting yourself, and that's okay. Manage your feelings and create a safe emotional environment for your daughter. Feeling the result of safeguarding your connection will ultimately be very soothing for both of you.

Home as the Free Zone

Teen girls benefit when their homes serve as a *free* zone. By free, I mean free from the pressures and opportunities to party, get high, and be sexual. Parents who think *Better in my home than out there somewhere* inadvertently create too much accessibility to behaviors that many girls take a pass on when availability is diminished. Home stops being safe when it is eliminated as the one free zone a teen girl has to escape the wild side. I have never seen a situation where the parents allowed getting high and having sex in the family home benefit a teen girl. I have, however, often seen this to be a detriment to the girl. With no barriers, teen girls find themselves over their heads in behaviors and activities that derail their healthy, balanced development.

What's the bottom line? Before teen girls develop clarity of values and boundaries, parents serve as auxiliary boundary keepers. As a parent, you can't protect your daughter from all the places and situations where she'll experience access to risky behaviors. You can, though, make the family home your daughter's free zone.

More Tips for Supporting Good Decisions

When it comes to raising teen girls, the more support the better. Here are a few more tips:

State expectations and give reminders. Give your daughter clear messages about risky behaviors. Let her know that the longer she waits to have sex and drink alcohol or use substances, the better for her brain and all other aspects of her functioning. If she's planning to have friends overnight, feel free to give reminders: "Honey, we know that our home is a free zone without drugs and alcohol. Make sure your friends are clear about that too."

Distinguish dangerous experimentation from typical experimentation: There are two general paths of experimenting with "partying" and sex. Typically teens who experiment are looking to have fun, develop identity and relationships, and try new behaviors. Their experimentation often creates minimal negative impact on their lives (social, familial, physical, emotional). More problematically, some teen girls are driven toward sex, drugs, and alcohol by emotional pain and/or trauma. In this case, they participate in sexual behavior or substance use full on, making choices that are reckless and impulsive, and that soon put them in danger.

Red flags include extreme mood and behavior changes, sudden and intense rages toward parents or old friends, coming home drunk or high, bladder infections and sexually transmitted diseases, refusal to go to school, and general withdrawal. Many parents and teens benefit from professional help in these high-risk situations. In a therapeutic environment, the feelings propelling the intensity of such behavior can be identified, ventilated, and worked through. Family members can get help structuring a plan to support the teen girl in getting back in the safe zone. Part of the plan might include the following tips:

Share news. The daily news regularly depicts real-life consequences of risk-taking behaviors. Your daughter may also know about real-life examples in your family or in your social circle. Openly discuss these situations whenever possible, and provide support and information when necessary.

Spend positive time. Even if your daughter makes choices that worry you, it still pays to spend positive time with her. You can be clear that her behavior isn't okay and even give consequences without placing her in emotional Siberia.

Check-in. Many teen girls spend hours alone each day. Too much time alone opens a huge loop your daughter can slip through. Keep in touch with her, tell her when you expect her to check in, make sure she knows where she needs to be, and by what time, every day. Better yet, make sure she has meaningful activities to absorb some of that alone time. Bump her way up on your radar but in a loving, not punitive, way.

All daughters need love. If your daughter walks on the wild side, she needs signs of your steadfast love even more than usual.

7

Achievement Stress Rescue

Teen girls are under a lot more academic stress than they used to be. Many factors contribute to this increase in pressure: a struggling national economy, a financially beleaguered educational system, a substantial increase in college applicants, greater opportunity and pressure to take advanced placement high school classes, and the fear that not performing puts you out of the game for scholarship money. With this pressure, it's not surprising that stress-related problems such as eating disorders, self-cutting, anxiety, and depression increasingly torment today's teen girls. Nor is it surprising that our overscheduled teen girls feel troubled by emotional pain such as feelings of emptiness, meaninglessness, anger, and loss of joy. If your daughter is affected by achievement stress, you may recognize some of the symptoms listed below.

You May Be Noticing:

- Much of her self-esteem seems contingent on achievement.

- All of her commitments involve a strong achievement/performance component.

- She doesn't seem to enjoy herself much of the time.

- She worries a lot about grades and performance.

- She craves sugar and caffeine.

- She seems to have a chronic, simmering anger punctuated by frequent or occasional "boilovers."

- She complains of sleeplessness, headaches, and stomachaches.

- She bursts into stress-induced crying spells.

- She's often irritable and doesn't seem to have effective coping strategies.

- She's seldom playful, creative, or joyful.

The list is long, but I produced it quickly because I see teens with one or more of these symptoms every day in my practice. Some want to convince themselves, and me, that they are "fine" with their relentless schedules and that they achieve because they want to. Others are clear that their lives are over-the-top stressful because of the pressure they feel from their parents, themselves, or outside forces.

This chapter will help you deal with your daughter's achievement stress in two ways:

1. You can safeguard your daughter's healthy, balanced development by understanding the difference between what is healthy and what is not.

2. You can determine whether or not you drive up her stress level. If you do, you'll get ideas to help you modify your behavior.

Stressed Out

In her 2006 book *Stressed-Out Girls*, Roni Cohen-Sandler notes that girls, more than boys, are affected by achievement stress. Why? Girls often believe that to be successful, they have to be *extraordinary* in every area of their lives: academic, social, extracurricular, and appearance. While boys tend to think of high school as a means to an end, girls are more likely to measure their success and self-worth based on what happens socially, emotionally, and academically every day! Disappointments that boys shrug off, girls take very personally. What's the icing on this stress "cake"? Girls hide their stress. They downplay and hide their suffering from parents in order to maintain autonomy, protect their parents from worry, and avoid both parental scrutiny and repercussions (Cohen-Sandler 2006). One girl said of her concern: "I want to tell my mom more about what's going on in my life, but having her involved will just give me more to stress about."

As a parent, you know that your daughter's achievement stress impacts more than just her. Parents, and even siblings, find themselves on a runaway train of commitments. Family evenings, weekends, even holidays are derailed by assigned projects, test preparation, homework, sports commitments, dance performances, and music recitals. Given the complexity of scheduling, skillful calendar management becomes crucial to family functioning. As families struggle to stay on track, parents are consumed with helping their teens navigate appointments, college prep checklists, carpools, uniform and gear organization, extra training and tutoring, snack packing, and places to be both in and out of town.

Danger Zone

Since teen girls are still developing positive coping strategies, they often shut down, explode, or become symptomatic in other ways (drugs, alcohol, self-harming, screen-time escapism, physical illnesses). Their identities and sense of value can be dangerously interwoven into their achievement status. Unremitting academic stress, combined with lack of sleep, inadequate identity development, and fear that their value is tied to their grades, makes some girls vulnerable to suicidal thoughts and behavior. As one fifteen-year-old put it, "I'm not sure why I did it. It seems stupid now, but at the time, I felt really overwhelmed and tired and in need of relief. So I ate a bunch of Tylenol and ended up in the hospital. It seemed like a viable option at the time. I couldn't think past the stress and fear of disappointing everyone."

This teen girl's parents were shocked by her suicide attempt. They acknowledged that academic performance and an emphasis on college dominated too much family conversation. Overlooked was her chronic lack of sleep, the many hours she spent on schoolwork in her room, her lack of exercise, her addiction to sugar and caffeine, and her chronic joylessness. If her parents had been given the behavior checklist above, they might have noticed that their daughter was in danger. Well-intended, her parents felt her struggles were in fact normal, inevitable, and even a necessary preparation for a successful life.

One sixteen-year-old dealt with her stress in another way. This radiant, high-achieving teen was sent to therapy when her parents became extremely worried about her binge drinking. She felt a lot of academic pressure from her father, who became angry when she received a B+ on a progress report. That pressure and her belief that his love was contingent upon her performance created deep pain and resentment in her. Well-intended, her father felt he was securing a good future for his bright and capable daughter. Instead, this gifted girl soothed her anger and pain with partying and dreams of moving far away from her dad.

Parents, like this girl's dad, want to support the highest good for their teen. A culture that screams ONLY ADVANCED PLACEMENT CLASSES AND STRAIGHT As ARE GOOD ENOUGH! YOUR FUTURE IS AT STAKE! sucks parents into the fear that drives unhealthy achievement. Sure, they notice their daughter seems anxious and joyless, but it has to be that way, right? Wrong.

Healthy Achievement vs. Unhealthy Achievement

Healthy achievement is motivated and sustained by a natural and authentic desire to learn and do one's best. Healthy achievers take pride in their accomplishments and enjoy engagement in a spectrum of interests and activities. They accept that not every test, paper, or project will get them an A, and they are more driven by internal interest, passion, and creativity than external validation, approval, and acceptance. They will risk going outside the box with their thinking and efforts because they have a sense of adventure and feel strongly about what they're working on, even if it doesn't get them the A+. While healthy achievers enjoy good grades, their self-esteem is not solely grade dependent. They make time to *live life now*. They are able to be playful, have fun, be creative, and maintain perspective.

> Unhealthy achievers have lost the love of learning in order to outrun failure.

In stark contrast, *unhealthy achievement* refers to the need for extraordinary performance in order to feel good enough to oneself and/or to one's teachers, parents, and/

or peer group. Unhealthy achievers believe only a few avenues to success exist and that life is a huge competition to access one of those avenues. These girls may have loved learning in the past, but they have lost the love of learning in order to outrun failure. Facing brutal competition for college admittance, they consider failure to be anything other than an A.

Sadly, unhealthy achievers must continually achieve and perform to maintain a feeling of being good enough and to keep pace with their rigorous schedule of commitments. Some teens consider cheating reasonable and necessary behavior since their education has become about grades instead of about engaging in the process of learning, growing, and nurturing passion. Unhealthy achievers are often very future focused and hold superficial notions about the meaning of success.

What Is Healthy, Balanced Development?

Teen girls are meant to be learning, growing, and developing along several progressive lines. If teen development were represented as your hand, each finger could symbolize a path of development. For example, if your thumb represents healthy achievement, alongside it would be emotional development, social development, life-skills development, and physical development. Each of these paths possesses individual features. For instance, physical development includes a teen girl's need for adequate sleep, exercise, and good nutrition. The life-skills path of development includes a teen girl's need to begin managing a budget, her own schedule, her own laundry, her appointments, and the needs of her pet. Of course, different families have different expectations, but the underlying idea is that teen girls are coached and guided by parents to further their development and their ability to function responsibly in a variety of areas that will support their healthy adulthood.

Now include your second hand to represent additional paths of development such as spirituality, community building, family, music, and art. Since interests and values vary from person to person and family to family, paths of development also vary.

In a child-friendly, balance-conscious reality, you and your daughter (as well as our culture and educational system) would recognize all these paths of development as valuable and synergistic. We would value the B student with a passion for music and fostering cats as much as we valued the 4.3 grade point average of the student challenging herself with a heavy course load of AP classes. Developing good, solid coping skills and making time to play, be creative, and contribute to the family and the community would be as significant as earning an A in AP physics and nailing the SAT. Instead of being buried in hours of homework after a long school day, a teen girl might come home and unwind by doing some art, pleasure reading, walking the family dog, helping her parents make dinner, and then do a reasonable amount of highly relevant homework designed to enhance or solidify her learning that day.

But we don't live in a child-friendly, balance-conscious reality. If you want balance for your child, you need to create it and protect it. Teachers and coaches, struggling with pressures of their own, won't do it for you or your daughter. In our current reality, it is accepted that teen girls *must* sacrifice or completely abandon their childhoods to achieve and perform.

Lopsided Development

In my private practice, most of my teen clients are high achievers. Some ask to come; others come because their parents realize that their daughter lacks basic coping skills. Emotional outbursts, anxiety attacks, and depression serve as red flags to parents.

With any luck, I meet girls in their sophomore year of high school. Unfortunately many girls don't seek help until the year before they leave for college, the summer before, or after they crash and burn in college. At these later points in development, parents are very concerned. Earlier they may have noticed a lack of emotional development but kept thinking it would somehow "fill in" at some point. It didn't, because she didn't have time for normal emotional development to occur.

In the last five years, I've seen a new trend. College graduates, very high achievers from very prestigious schools, enter therapy depressed and angry. These young women talk about having done everything right, having jumped through every possible achievement hoop, only to be unemployed or underemployed in a bad economy, with their worried parents paying for their therapy and student loans. Many of these young women numb their feelings of pain, loss, and confusion with drugs and alcohol. Since many skipped a lot of fun that is supposed to go with being a teenager, they try and recapture those years through late nights of partying. In therapy, part of their work is grieving the childhood they sacrificed on the altar of achievement. In their early or mid-twenties, they are emotionally, creatively, and spiritually lost or underdeveloped.

Then and Now: How We Got Here

What's changed since parents were in high school? A lot! Many of today's teen girls laugh at the 4.0 grade point average that was the gold standard when their parents were in high school. Advanced placement classes, which involve more time, work, and pressure, expand the grade scale to 5.0, enabling girls to graduate with a grade point average exceeding 4.0.

When parents were in high school, they began seriously thinking about college in their junior year. Not anymore. Strike up a conversation with a middle school girl and you may find she already feels pressure about what she needs to do to get into college. Part of her confusion may be caused by what she has observed in her own community and perhaps in her own family. Many well-educated and trained professionals who held jobs that offered a degree of financial security now find themselves "downsized" and unemployed. Students feel pressure to achieve academically in order to compete in an uncertain economy, and they must do this in schools where cuts in state and federal funding mean fewer course selections, bigger class sizes, more years in college, and fewer teachers and support staff.

As early as kindergarten, five-year-olds are expected to accomplish academic tasks that were part of their parents' first- and second-grade curriculum. One retired kindergarten teacher, who worked in the public school system for more than thirty years, shares this observation:

I recently spent three days substituting in a kindergarten class. That was all I could take. The joyful, developmentally appropriate environment of just a few years before was gone. There were no large painting easels in the room. There was no children's art on the walls. The children knew no songs, no finger plays, no games. Instead of learning experientially, children were required to sit at tables for long periods of time doing math problems they couldn't begin to understand. The reading and writing tasks were similar. More than one child cried in frustration.

Good News: Challenge Success

A Stanford organization called Challenge Success is a collection of experts who formed a research and intervention project aimed at making school a healthier learning experience for students. At conferences that are widely attended by parents and educators, experts broaden public awareness about the dangers of excessive academic pressure and a narrow definition of success. The goal of Challenge Success is to work on site with schools to promote better health, engagement with learning, and integrity through changes such as

- creating better homework policies,

- making homework reasonable and meaningful,

- creating new assessment practices, and

- making changes in school schedules to give students time to integrate and reflect on learning.

At the 2008 Challenge Success Conference, founder Denise Pope stated that the irony of pushing kids so hard is that the business world often finds today's college grads inadequately prepared to meet the needs of our global economy. They lack creativity, leadership, adaptability, and strong communication skills. The strict emphasis on academic achievement serves neither the student nor the workforce (Pope 2008). Indeed, it makes intuitive sense that producing burned-out, passionless, hoop jumpers will fail to bring innovation and vitality to our dynamic global economy. More information about Challenge Success programs and research is available at challengesuccess.org.

Do You Contribute to Your Teen's Stress?

Are you a factor in your daughter's achievement stress? While many unhealthy achievers claim they are self-driven, it's often because they have unconsciously absorbed and internalized messages from parents, peers, their academically rigorous environment, or a super-achieving sibling. (If you have a Stanford decal on your car, you don't have to *tell* your daughter you expect her to get into Stanford for her to feel the pressure.) Even if a teen girl has completely different aptitudes and interests than a sibling (or parent), she may struggle with efforts to measure up.

Parents are sometimes aware they push their daughters but feel it is necessary to ensure success. Other parents are unaware that they are exerting pressure and setting punishing expectations. They are bewildered when their angry achievers go subterranean and participate in risky behaviors to express and release their anger and/or numb their pain.

If you've been affected by the culture of fear that drives unhealthy achievement, you may identify with the following. Do you

○ worry a lot about your daughter getting into the "right" college?

○ ask her more about her grades than about what she's learning and how she thinks and feels about what she's learning?

○ bribe her to get good grades?

○ look the other way when she isn't getting enough sleep or enough free time, because you believe there's no other choice?

○ ask, "Did you win?," "What grade did you get on…?," or "How did you do?," instead of inviting her to tell you about it?

Exercise: Supporting Healthy Development

If you recognize yourself in any of the above behaviors, you can make changes that benefit your daughter's healthy development. For example, one parent decided to stop checking her daughter's grades online. Instead, she let her daughter know that her grades were up to her and that she was willing to support her daughter in any way requested.

Are you a factor in your daughter's achievement stress? Is there anything you'd like to change?

_____

_____

_____

What would you like to do instead?

_____

_____

_____

What are the benefits you hope to see?

_____

_____

_____

Conveying Healthy Messages

Teen girls absorb more of our messages and attitudes than they let on. What we convey explicitly and implicitly makes an impact. See if the following messages work for you. If they do, try conveying them to your daughter.

Grades don't determine worth. One parent gave her daughter a mantra to say to herself when stressed: "I am not my grade." Another parent lightened the load of her stressed-out daughter by reminding and supporting her to focus on her process of preparation more than the grade.

The point of high school is to learn and grow as a person. Help your daughter achieve perspective by telling her that you value her exposure to, and interest in, a variety of topics and activities. This shows her she is more to you and the world than a set of grades or accomplishments.

You value her efforts more than her grades. When you comment more on her efforts than on the results of her efforts, you support her in being process driven instead of outcome driven. She needs to know that no matter how hard she works, she's not going to rock every test and assignment, and that's okay. Here are some examples:

○ Outcome comment: "What grade did you get on that assignment?"

○ Process comment: "You're really thinking creatively about this assignment."

○ Outcome comment: "How did you place in your volleyball tournament?"

○ Process comment: "Tell me about the volleyball tournament."

○ Teen making an outcome comment: "Mom! My Spanish test was so hard and unfair! She put stuff on that test we haven't even talked about!"

○ Mom responding with a process comment: "I've seen the energy you've put into that class, and I think you should feel good about your efforts. Also, your Spanish is getting better and better."

You're excited she's learning more about the world and her place in it. Ask her to share some of what she's learning with you. Show interest in her learning experience, not just her grades.

There are many good colleges, not just a few. If she's fixated on a couple of top-tier choices, let her know that you feel it's more about what she makes of her college experience than the college itself. If she's a junior, check out the College Board website (www.collegeboard.org) for information on colleges. You can also visit different campuses with your daughter. You'll learn more about the schools, and your girl will see that there's life beyond high school. You're also likely to create some fun memories while you're gathering information and she's imagining herself in college!

It's ridiculous for anyone to expect to be extraordinary at everything. Encourage your daughter's irreverence to that suffocating notion. At some point, most adults replace performance anxiety with self-acceptance. It's very freeing. Share your wisdom.

Honesty, kindness, compassion (add your own) are characteristics you value highly. Living and loving life is important. Lace these values into everyday conversations. Your teen daughter listens to you more than you think. If you value a sense of humor or admire people who live in the now instead of in their heads, share those values with your daughter. Model living and loving life now for your daughter.

> Model living and loving life now for your daughter.

Sometimes you reach for something, don't get it, and end up with something even better. Sometimes disappointments end up being huge gifts. Sometimes life has more in store for us than we plan for ourselves. Do you have a story you can share with your daughter about one door closing and another one opening? No matter who you are and how hard you work, you will experience surprise outcomes due to factors beyond your control, and that's part of the magic of life.

Predict your daughter's future success. Teen girls become livid in the face of comments such as "Oh my gosh, Brynn! How are you ever going to make it in college if you can't even keep track of your assignments now!" Predict success by saying things like "Wherever you end up going to college, you're going to do great! You're becoming more competent and independent all the time."

Tell your daughter that you just plain love her, no matter what. Teen girls bask in the warmth of this message, even if they appear to shrug it off. It's especially meaningful when they feel their parents love who they truly are, not just what they accomplish. As one daughter said (with a huge, proud smile), "My mom thinks I'm the funniest person on earth. I can make her laugh even when she's pissed at me."

Involving Your Daughter: A Check-In on Achievement Stress

Hopefully you're feeling more aware of achievement stress and how it may have affected you and your daughter. You now have ideas about how to start thinking, communicating, and behaving differently. To know how you're doing and what to focus on, why not offer a quick check-in?

Tell your daughter that you're interested in looking at the achievement stress she's under, and that you want to support her more and help reduce her stress. Ask her to help you see your role more clearly by answering five quick questions. Make sure to let her know you will not argue with any of her answers. You will simply use the information to create more awareness regarding your role in her achievement stress.

1. I feel a lot of pressure from my parent(s) to get good grades.

2. I feel my parent(s) want me to do my best, but they are reasonable and supportive.

3. I feel that less than exceptional grades will disappoint my parent(s).

4. I feel my parent(s) care more about me as a person than as an achiever.

5. I feel like my parent(s) love me no matter what.

No matter what you learn, thank your daughter for her cooperation and use the feedback to make helpful adjustments..

Feedback Conversations

If it feels right and your daughter seems open, ask her what she'd like you to do differently. To make opening up to you a good experience,

o   do listen with your heart;

o   do validate what she shares; and

o   do accept her words as gold nuggets that you value and take seriously.

Example of a "do": "I can see how my constant reminders feel like nagging to you." As you listen, no matter what,

- don't blow it by getting combative or defensive;

- don't explain yourself or make excuses; and

- don't take over the conversation or steer it in any other direction.

Example of a "don't": "You think I'm overbearing, but if you'd take more responsibility for your time management, I could back off. What we really need to talk about is…" Such comments drive teen girls crazy because they perceive the parent as not listening or being accountable. If giving you feedback isn't a positive experience, your relationship will suffer because she will withhold feedback in the future. When you handle feedback well, you model openness, nurture closeness and trust, and transform information into new behavior. Your daughter gets to experience herself as worth listening to, which establishes a sense of confidence and positive identity—hugely important for her as she moves into her adult life!

Here's how one teen and her mom navigated a feedback discussion:

Rosa: Okay. You want to know what I think you could do differently. Well, the first thing you asked me after school today was if I got my chem test back. That kind of question stresses me out! I'm already stressed and that makes me more stressed. And you keep bringing up taking the SAT again. I'm still recovering from the last time.

Parent: I can see how my questions affect you that way. What would you like me to do differently next time?

Rosa: Just trust me. I'm doing my best. Sometimes I study really hard, but the test is crazy and that teacher asks stuff we haven't even covered! No matter what my grade is, you'll know eventually. Maybe I don't want to talk about it right away. And I know I have to take the SAT again. I can handle it myself.

Parent: I get it. And you don't need one speck more stress from me. I'm going to try to be more aware of how I accidentally cause more stress for you. I will work on trusting that you are doing your best and pull back on asking and reminding. I'm also going to trust that you will tell me if you need some additional support. Thanks for being willing to help me with this. Like you, I'm still figuring things out about life.

Getting Help for Risky Behavior

If you suspect your daughter is self-cutting, bingeing and purging, starving, compulsively exercising, binge drinking, shoplifting, using drugs, or participating in other dangerous behaviors, *seek help.* She is attempting to regulate her emotional turmoil with these behaviors. Many of these behaviors are very *self-reinforcing*, which means they "work" in that they help her discharge or numb her suffering. Your daughter can learn new and better ways to cope—and it's important that she learn them now. Her lifestyle also must be reconstructed so it is conducive to her healthy development. She'll need to decrease the *have to's* and increase her *get to's* so she feels her life is her own and that she's more that an accomplishment machine.

More Tips for Stress Relief

To protect teen girls from achievement stress burnout, we parents can keep an eye on stress levels and support our girls in rebalancing. Here are some ideas:

Playtime. Your daughter needs time for play. Be her fun monitor and make sure she's having enough. Movie nights with friends, baking, hiking, bowling, roller skating, board games, and the like can do wonders for her. Remember how you used to pick up inexpensive little toys for her when she was little? She probably still enjoys bubbles, Smashball, or sidewalk chalk.

Schedule review. Check in regularly with your daughter about her schedule. Help her identify things she can curtail or eliminate in order to have more free time. Help her examine her reasons for engaging in all her commitments so she can begin to evaluate her "have to–get to" ratio. Remind her she needs to put some fun and rest into every day in order to be happy and healthy. See chapter 10 for an exercise—"On Track with Happiness"—to help you with schedule review.

Reinforce her IS-ness. Let her know you adore who she is, not what she does. Remind her she is a human "being" and not a human "doing." Help her feel good about resting and playing and just plain BE-ing. Leading by example is a very powerful way to teach and honor rest and play, so do it in your own life.

> Help her feel good about resting and playing and just plain BE-ing.

Seek reinforcement. If your daughter struggles in school, she may have a learning difference that needs to be identified and accommodated. If she generally does well but struggles in a particular class, subject, or study skill, consult with the teacher and/ or school counselor about it. Teachers and counselors often have great ideas that can help ease your daughter's stress or support her improvement. Consider alternative solutions such as taking an online trig class instead of expecting your daughter to survive a poor teacher. If you can get a study hall in her schedule, seriously consider it. I've seen girls noticeably lighten up when they've had the opportunity to get some homework done during their school day.

Special care in senior year. The senior year, and often the junior year, can be very stressful for high achievers. They process more than we can possibly wrap our heads and hearts around. Even though they may seem to want to leave us, they also fear separation from us, which stirs a whole range of emotional responses. It's a good time to be very sensitive and emotionally attuned.

If this chapter helps you think differently about your daughter's achievement stress, your daughter is lucky! You're supporting and protecting her healthy development.

8

Taming the Tech Tiger

You were prepared for the sleep deprivation, teething, and terrible twos of your daughter's early years. You were both challenged and charmed by the poignant transitions of her elementary school years. You did your best ushering her through the ups and downs of her middle school years. But somewhere in the mix, an unexpected aspect of her development announced itself earlier than expected. It sounded something like this: "Mom, Dad, I want a cell phone. I neeeed a cell phone!"

You May Be Noticing:

○ Her phone seems to be surgically implanted into her hand. When it's not in her hand, it's (please, not again) LOST!

○ She appears to have Olympic capabilities in texting. (You suspect a Darwinian adaptation has facilitated mind-blowing leaps in thumb dexterity.)

○ Your scant alone time with her is regularly corrupted by a third party: her phone.

○ She checks her social networking site like a new mother checks her baby's breathing—with a certain primitive desperation.

How You Got Here

Technology may have entered your daughter's life with walkie-talkies or a karaoke machine. But soon came big-ticket tech items such as the MP3 player, the cell phone, and maybe even a laptop computer. Interactive video games became so brilliant, some of your daughter's gifts felt like presents for the whole family. While you may dabble in a little virtual tennis, let's face it: your daughter's tech savvy smashes yours right out of the court. Indeed, you received no warning, nor were you prepared for the speedy technological developments she masters effortlessly.

With enormous appetites for fast communication, information, and entertainment, teen girls present brand-new challenges for unprepared parents. Here's what some parents say about their tech-savvy teens:

o Is it even healthy for girls to be communicating as much as they do? When I was my daughter's age, I came home and got a break! Between texting, IM'ing, and Facebook, my daughter is constantly communicating.

o My daughter's mood can drop like a rock after being on Facebook. Then I have to deal with an upset kid who just found something out she didn't need to know in the first place.

o I heard my daughter and her friend laughing one evening and assumed they were watching a movie. I found out they were on some site that allowed them to video chat with complete strangers! They had no idea why I hit the roof.

Late to the Tech Party

When your daughter learned to access and watch entertainment via the Internet, she probably didn't consult you on her media choices. When she set up a Facebook account, she didn't necessarily ask your permission. When she accessed music for free, she probably left you out of the loop. By now, the toothpaste is so far out of the tube, you don't know how to scoop it back in. And, of course, you know any effort to do so won't be pretty: "*You* want to be my Facebook friend? You're kidding, right?"

Our late arrival at the tech party has created a difficult situation for us parents: many kids have unrestricted freedom, while we feel confused as to what's going on and how to get involved. In fact, only three in ten young people report having rules for how much time they spend watching TV, playing video games, or using the computer. In families where rules are set, teens spend significantly less time using media (Lamontagne 2010). So what should a parent do?

While there's no single approach to setting rules and monitoring media use, you can adjust your level of involvement to benefit your daughter's individual needs. For example, if you have a precocious thirteen-year-old with a ravenous appetite for socializing, high parental involvement and clear boundaries will be crucial. If you have an older teen who demonstrates good judgment in her life and already knows the ups and downs of technology, you may choose to be less vigilant. Let's take on the biggest tech tigers one at a time so you'll feel more confident guiding your daughter.

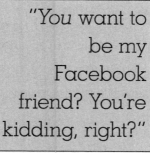

"You want to be my Facebook friend? You're kidding, right?"

Tiger #1: Cell Phones

Teen girls *love* their cell phones, with ownership increasing massively every year. While parents crave a break from phone communication, teen girls can't seem to get enough. Although many girls have smart phones with pricey media packages to access the Internet, cell phones are really about something else. One teen girl explained: "It's about the TEXTING!" Their texting prowess and hunger are impressive—and unfathomable.

The Upside of Cell Phones

Cell phones give parents easy access to their daughters. Gone are the days when you called the Jones household to summon your teen home. Cell phones provide a straight line from parent to child, which allows parents to check in easily. Not surprisingly, teen girls often endure these check-ins dramatically. As a result, many parents have taken on the texting challenge in order to communicate in short sound bites:

Don't forget orthodontist today after school! or *Good luck at practice today. See you at dinner.* ☺ But sometimes... *Are you really at the movies? Take a picture of yourself on the way out and send it to me.*

When parents give out consequences for unwanted behavior, they often take away or limit their daughter's cell phone use. They find it an effective way to get her attention and make an impact. It's an especially appropriate consequence if parents find out their daughter misuses her phone. If she sends or receives inappropriate texts or you learn about dangerous or concerning behavior through reading her texts, a phone restriction effectively gives her time away from communicating to discuss the issues with you, a trusted family friend or relative, or a professional.

The Downside of Cell Phones

For many parents, cell phones interrupt family time, cause concern about quality and quantity of communication, raise concern about driving safety, and create a financial burden. For teen girls, the downside of cell phone use is potential overcommunication, irresponsible communication, overstimulation, distraction, disrupted and diminished sleep, and increased risk of car accidents. Indeed, many teen girls sleep with their phone under their pillows. No wonder they're tired!

SET LIMITS: PREPARE FOR FALLOUT

If you've never put limits on your daughter's cell phone use, prepare yourself. When your daughter blows up, stay calm and focused. Since we all want our feelings or our point acknowledged (almost as much as we want to get our way), make sure to acknowledge her while also standing firm with your request: "I get it, Amy—this seems especially unfair because I've never asked you to do this before. I don't blame you for being upset. Still, this is our new rule: your phone goes in the basket, ringer off, during dinner and at bedtime. When you honor this rule, you will get it back in the morning."

Deciding on appropriate limits can be challenging. The ideas below reflect parental efforts to set cell phone limits:

- We created a cell phone–use policy that my daughter signed. It states that she must have her phone charged and with her so we can reach her. It also states her use limits and her commitment to pay if limits are exceeded. Finally, it states we can access her phone if and when we feel a need to.

- We purchased a limited texting plan until she could show us that texting wasn't interfering with her schoolwork. She is much more discerning about her texting now.

NO HALL PASS FOR PARENTS

Take a moment to think about your own cell phone use. Your daughter has a long history of seeing your face light up when you see her. While it may seem she doesn't give a darn about that anymore, she does care. A lot. In a subtle but crucial way, you make her feel safe in her whacky world. Don't let your cell phone interfere with that.

And, of course, we teach our kids by example. We must therefore stop being phone "sneakers." We can't tell our daughters "I'm just checking the time" when we're really checking an incoming call. Being a good example can stress us (for example, when we want to sneak in a quick text at a long red light) or motivate us (for example, to pull to the side of the road before answering an important work-related call). Try to make better decisions, knowing that your choices affect your daughter.

Ask your daughter how she feels about your cell phone use. Listen carefully—and nondefensively. Here's what two girls say about their feelings:

- It really annoys me when I get to the car only to see my mom absorbed on her Crackberry. I know it's stupid, but it hurts my feelings.

- My parents think their addiction to their smart phones is okay because it's "work related." I always come in second to the phone.

When your daughter sees that her feedback impacts your cell-phone behavior, she feels a sense of self-worth and importance. She knows you value her feedback and take her feelings seriously. This respectful communication can benefit both you and your daughter.

Safety Tips for Cell Phone Use

To maximize cell phone safety for your daughter, here are a few tips:

Create a car-starting routine. Have your daughter create a routine before she starts the car that involves putting her cell phone (ringer off) out of reach. This should be as automatic as buckling her seatbelt and checking her mirrors. Putting the phone in a glove box or, better yet, the backseat will prevent your driving teen from using or checking her phone. Help her perfect her commitment by riding with her until you see her safety routine is ingrained.

Check her phone anytime. Let her know you can check her phone anytime. This is especially important for young teens. A teen girl's assumption that her phone should be private is mistaken. She's a child and requires parental guidance until she has the maturity and life experience to make sound decisions. If you read any unkind, insensitive, or inappropriate texting being sent, received, or forwarded, have a short talk about cyberbullying. (This will be covered later in this chapter.)

Learn how to decode texting lingo. Check out www.netlingo.com or the iPhone app called LRNtheLingo. Many teen girls, however, don't disguise text content with lingo. Aside from a BTW here and an LMAO there, most parents are more challenged by deciphering the spelling than the lingo. (Interestingly many teen girls don't think to erase incriminating content from their text log.)

You learned new ideas and skills for talking to your teen daughter in chapter 4. Here's a new strategy for briefly and effectively addressing any important topic.

The Ten-Minute Talk

When it comes to cell phones, we parents must claim a few teaching moments. For several reasons related to normal, healthy development, teen girls are pros at resisting such parental encounters. Put your daughter at ease by setting a ten-minute limit and sticking to it. When you tell her you need to talk to her *for only ten minutes,* she will feel less trapped. She will be in a better position to suck it up and allow the conversation to unfold.

Sexting, a touchy topic, refers to sending or receiving sexually explicit texts and/or nude or nearly nude images. While sexting has received a lot of media attention, many teens say they have not sent or received sexually explicit messages. Those girls who say they have are usually older teens who send pictures or provocative texts to their romantic partner. If the subject of sexting makes your heart speed up a bit, it's because we parents instantly recognize the inherent risk of such communication. Unlike our teen daughters, our brain development is complete and we have the life experience to forecast negative outcomes. Teen girls sext because they fail to anticipate the harm that can result from such behavior. One teen girl shares her experience: "I felt a little awkward sending the photo, but this guy talked me into it. He kept texting me and asking for something really special, like it would be a present, so I did it. Then he sent it to about fifty other kids, who sent it to even more kids. I had to switch schools to escape being called a whore and a slut."

SAMPLE TEN-MINUTE SEXT TALK

Even though your daughter may wince when you bring up the topic of safe texting, practice your communication skills with your version of the following conversation. Of course, you will tailor your ten-minute talk to suit your style.

Katy, I want to talk to you about a phone safety issue that's been in the news lately. It will only take ten minutes, even less if you can give me your full attention. You probably already know this, but I need to say it just because I'm your parent and it's my job to guide you and keep you safe when I can. Never say, text, or send anything you wouldn't want the world to know or see. There are girls who have been really hurt when sexual texting got forwarded or shared with others. Girls who participate in sexting are not necessarily "bad" or "slutty" girls. They learn really humiliating and painful lessons, and I never want you to go through that. If you ever find yourself in a bad situation of any kind, remember I love and support you. Know that you can always come to me for help.

Whenever possible, remind your teen that no "mistake" can separate her from your love and support. She needs more support when she blows it, not less.

Here's an important legal note: Beyond social and emotional consequences, sexting for minors still falls under child pornography laws in many states. Therefore, if your daughter takes a nude picture of herself and sends it electronically, this may be considered child pornography. If your daughter receives a nude image and forwards the message, this may be considered the distribution of child pornography. Some cases of sexting land teens on the registered sex offender's list. Make sure your daughter knows the potential legal consequences.

> She needs more support when she blows it, not less.

In your ten-minute talk, you may find that your daughter is open to answering a few questions such as "What do you think or know about sexting?" or "Why do you think girls send sexts?" After about ten minutes, thank her for the conversation and move on. If ten minutes isn't enough, you can revisit the topic another day. Plan your follow-up thoughts and questions so you stay succinct and productive. When you resist overtalking, you prove to your daughter that talking to you isn't a swamp from which she'll never emerge.

You can further limit your actual talking time by having her research the topic with or without your involvement. Teens are skilled Internet researchers and would rather receive information from sources other than parents. You may also suggest your daughter consult an expert or other resource to get information on sexting. She can share with you an abbreviated version of what she learned. With these approaches, your daughter drives her learning moment while you offer a little direction from the backseat.

Tiger #2: The Internet

The upside and downside of using the Internet are the same: the Internet allows access to the world! Whether conducting research for school assignments, obtaining factoids on a new band or hot actor, checking the weather in Brazil, locating the highest rated cookie recipe, or keeping in touch with friends through social networking sites, teen girls navigate the Internet with the ease we parents navigate our path to the shower.

Choosing Sites Carefully

The skill teen girls demonstrate in navigating the Web is also a call for caution. While the Internet can be a great resource, not everything found online is true. This is not news to teen girls, who have probably already been warned by their parents and teachers that hundreds of information sources, including Wikipedia, are not necessarily credible or accurate. There are also numerous websites requesting money for things that are not real. One such hoax is Save the Tree Octopus, when in fact there's no such thing as a tree octopus, but you can still send money to save the nonexistent creatures.

To make sure your daughter is discerning about her online sources, ask her how she knows a website is reliable. If your tone is curious instead of accusatory, she will be open instead of defensive. Find out what she looks for when choosing a site or a source. If she is unsure, suggest she check with her teacher for tips that will help her identify trustworthy sources.

Dealing with Disturbing Content

Teen girls know that, without trying, they come across inappropriate, sexual, or disturbing content as they surf the Web. Take a few minutes to discuss this: "You know, Maggie, I run into some pretty freaky stuff on the Internet sometimes. What do you do when that happens to you?"

Many girls will laugh and agree or throw out an "Oh, Mom!" or "Oh, Dad!" Persist in order to assess whether or not your daughter knows how to respond. If she does, express appreciation for her good thinking. If she doesn't, or if your assessment is foiled by her avoidance of the conversation, let her know in a calm, direct manner that she will someday encounter inappropriate content.

Warn her that just about anything and everything can be found on the Internet and, not only is there no benefit to seeing it, it can be upsetting. Even a seemingly harmless search can present Internet users with unwanted material. Communicate your expectation that she avoid clicking on sketchy sites or exit immediately when she encounters one.

Password Protection

Password protection is an example of a safety issue that your daughter may think she's got covered but really doesn't. While teen girls know to keep their passwords private, they may not know to treat security questions as second passwords. Most accounts require users to provide answers to "security questions" in the event that the password is forgotten. Tell your daughter she needs to treat the security question as she would a second password—that is, pick a security question that only she can answer. Otherwise her accounts can be easily hacked by anyone who is motivated to do the scant research necessary to answer the security question. The more visible and active your daughter is online, the greater the opportunity she will attract the attention of someone willing to do that research.

If you are a parent who believes in online privacy for your daughter, have her write all of her passwords and accounts down on a piece of paper that goes into a sealed envelope. In case of emergency, you can access the information. This safety tip has actually saved lives.

Communicate Expectations

Articulating expectations over and over again is the bread and butter of parenting your teen. You can't make sure that all of her behavior will meet your expectations, but you can make sure she knows what they are. After all, it's not as though we teach our children to say "Please" and "Thank you" one time and it sticks forever. We repeat it over and over again. We need to do the same with expectations about online behavior. If we don't repeat our rules and expectations, teen girls will forget them and generate their own.

Among other things, teen girls use the Internet to access music, movies, and television shows. To ensure your teen's safety and well-being, communicate standards for movie and television viewing on a regular basis. If your daughter uses the computer in a family living space, you can unobtrusively check her viewing to ensure her choices align with your standards.

Invite your daughter to share her music with you and the family from time to time. If she is not comfortable sharing her music choices, you may want to review lyrics and messages contained in the music. This is another opportunity to communicate your values and standards. This is how one parent monitors music: "I have random check-ins with Rosie's music. I make it very clear to her that if the lyrics or message would offend me or any other self-respecting woman, the music goes! In addition, my daughter will have to endure a rant from me about the internalized oppression of women in our culture."

Use-Risk Factor

As your daughter's Internet use rises, her activity on multiple sites and applications might also rise. Depending on how she's using those sites, her risk of being harmed by people known and unknown may also increase. To secure safety for your daughter, let's take on Tiger #3.

Tiger #3: Social Networking

Even the least techy of parents knows what social networking is. Facebook is ubiquitous in the lives of teen girls, and many parents enjoy it as well. Soon Facebook will be joined by sites with all video-based communication, which some consider the next social networking frontier.

The Upside of Social Networking

With social networking, your daughter has the ability to stay in touch and get immediate updates from her friends while making new connections. For teens who are socially less connected than they desire to be, social networking can help them meet friends of friends and develop a social network. For mature girls who have a light relationship to social networking, the upside is staying in touch and pure enjoyment. Some parents create a social networking account and "friend" their daughter. They appreciate the ability to get insight into the relationships and dynamics important in their teen's life.

The Downside of Social Networking

Three notable downsides to social networking are distraction, drama, and danger. Let's take a closer look at each of them.

Distraction. Many parents notice an addictive aspect to teen-girl social networking. Grades may suffer, as do in-person relationship building and communication skills. Social-networking teens may narrow their scope of interests and activities in order to spend more time on Facebook and other sites. Parents need to ensure balance when teen girls dip too heavily into the world of cybercommunication.

Drama. Parents also notice that social networking creates havoc in the teen social realm. It's extremely hard for an adult to fully comprehend how oblivious teen girls can be regarding what they post. Sensitive, kind girls can become very insensitive; sensible girls can show shocking lapses in judgment.

Teen girls don't always understand that what they say and post (a) reflects on them and (b) impacts others, often traumatically. They are often surprised when their posts hurt feelings, destroy relationships, and ruin reputations. Some may even be shocked at long-term consequences when academic scholarships, awards, or college admittance are affected by what they post online. More commonly, employers are on social networking sites and use the information they find to make hiring decisions.

Because the communication is not face-to-face, teen girls feel they have complete freedom to say anything. When someone posts an unkind comment about someone else, several people can dog-pile on top of the initial comment, inflaming and escalating the trajectory of harm. Since nothing is truly private, people get really, really hurt. One parent has this to say about this type of communication: "A lot of drama happens on social networking! These kids don't filter anything they say. I sensed a lot of turmoil in my daughter's social life and finally insisted she give me her password. She and her "Facebook friends" were swearing, harassing each other, and referencing sex and alcohol. Some of the girls were posting photos of themselves that would give their parents a heart attack. My daughter insists none of it is a big deal, but I think that's the problem!"

Why so audacious? Your developing teen girl is exploring identity formation. She isn't always sure who she is or what her values are. She may want to explore what it feels like to be edgy, sexually powerful, or socially aggressive. This may lead to online behavior that makes you wonder, *Who are you and what have you done with my daughter?* Some naive teen girls post pictures, make comments to others, and engage in gossip or harassment in ways that reflect their undeveloped judgment—their identity of the month—and their obliviousness to the potential impact of such online behavior. Since their online communication is immediate, a comment or photo can turn into a colossal social trauma or reputation-maker/breaker in literally seconds.

Danger. The last and potentially most serious downside to social networking is danger. Teen girls do fall prey to bullies and predators. For the need-to-know on this topic, I spoke to Internet safety expert Lori Getz, founder of Cyber Education Consultants.

According to Lori Getz, avoid these three things in your cyber social life: over-friending, oversharing, and overconnecting. These three Os make girls more visible, and too much visibility can be dangerous.

Overfriending means inviting someone into your online life whom you wouldn't have at your dinner table. Teen girls can be very trusting and naive. Overfriending leads to trusting people girls hardly know or don't know at all.

Oversharing refers to posting information such as your upcoming trip to Hawaii. Teen girls also commonly post emotional personal information that bullies or predators can access.

Overconnecting is communicating on multiple sites and applications, often using the same user name. Such teens call attention to themselves on sites like YouTube, Hot or Not, or Chat Roulette. The more your daughter is out there, the more attention she receives. While some attention is wanted, other attention can be devastating or dangerous. Having the same user name across sites makes her easy to search and target. Emotionally vulnerable girls are targets for predators, while highly visible girls are targets for bullies.

While all three Os are distinct, they also overlap and interact. For example, teen girls love to feel loved, and many "friend" people they barely know or have never met (overfriending). This practice escalates risk, especially when it interacts with oversharing and overconnecting. Let's say Jessica has two hundred friends. Being a communicative teen, she shares information including photos of herself and her packing list for Hawaii. Even if Jessica doesn't post info about her upcoming trip, one of her friends may "comment" her with a quick "Aloha, Jess. Have fun in Hawaii!" Now the information is out there and Jessica is more visible, more searchable, more vulnerable—and the family home may be targeted for robbery or vandalism.

Oversharing can also take the form of a frustrated teen posting *I hate my parents* on her wall. You may be fine with this expression of frustration. But if she's also overconnecting on multiple sites, remember that she's more visible to more people. A bully or a predator may become interested in her. If she hates her parents, a predator may identify her as a possible target. He then sets up a profile to bait her into a relationship. With little effort, he can become an expert on her. He saw her on YouTube, knows what she looks like, who her friends are, where she hangs out, that her boyfriend just dumped her. If you're starting to get really creeped out, you're not alone!

> Don't be afraid to have her shave down her Internet activity.

What's the bottom line? Talk to your daughter about the three Os and review her standing on all three. Provide her with articles about what has happened to other girls. Touch base with her frequently about her online activities. Don't be afraid to have her shave down her Internet activity.

More Tips on Social Networking

Many parents respond creatively to social networking in order to provide damage control. Here are some of their ideas:

o   My daughter uses a computer in family living space so complete privacy is prevented or limited.

o   We installed filtering and monitoring software.

o   I use my daughter's password to access her site. Initially I thought being her "friend" was enough. Then I found out that she was selectively blocking me from information she didn't want me to see. Having her password allows me to view everything and therefore monitor everything.

o My daughter learned to restrain her social networking activity when I imposed a posthomework, one-hour time limit.

o I had my daughter close her social networking accounts completely. Her judgment proved to be too undeveloped, and the consequences of her communication have been too damaging.

Exercise: Inventory Her Sites

Learn the sites your daughter spends time on. Let her know you don't want to be intrusive, but you must be involved. Remind her that she gets more freedom when you know she's cooperative, knowledgeable, sensible, and safe. Log the information below and use it later to help you remember what you're monitoring.

Site   **Password**

_____   _____

_____   _____

_____   _____

_____   _____

Follow-up questions you can ask your daughter:

o What do you like about this site?

o What don't you like about it?

o How do you avoid problems?

o How do you handle disrespectful or hurtful comments?

If your daughter's posts or communication reveals content that is inappropriate, respond carefully. If you flip out, she may firewall you from her cyberlife by becoming more subterranean in her activities. Limit your comments as much as possible and ask her to give you more information about troubling material.

Cyberbullying

Some people perceive bullying as "age-old, just a normal part of growing up." But there is nothing normal or acceptable about victimization, especially now that the problem has jumped from the hallways to the world stage with the speed of a cyber-bullet. Chapter 9 will provide support on how to deal with bullying, but we'll explore cyberbullying here.

Common forms of *cyberbullying* involve using the Internet, cell phones, social networking sites, or other electronic means to send or forward mean messages, post pictures of victims without their consent, or spread lies and rumors about victims. Often it involves a bully pretending to be another person online. The consequences of cyberbullying can be devastating and result in anxiety, depression, loss of sleep or appetite, and damage to school performance. Cyberbullies can drive a teen girl into suicidal despair. Since teen girls don't always tell parents when they're being bullied, take note if your daughter seems upset, sleepless, anxious, depressed, fearful, or withdrawn. If you learn she is a victim of online bullying, here's how you can help:

- Encourage her to delete messages without reading them.

- If she does read an intimidating message, tell her not to respond. Instead, encourage her to print out the entire conversation and tell someone she trusts—you, a friend, a school counselor—about the cyberbully.

- Keep computers in a central location where messages can be monitored.

- Make sure she "unplugs" before bed and leaves her cell phone outside her room. Many aggressive messages are sent in the middle of the night. Teen girl sleepovers are convenient for reckless online behavior.

○ Find out how to report online abuse to your Internet service provider or website moderator.

○ If your teen is threatened online, contact local law enforcement.

As with all wildlife, always treat tech tigers with wary respect. They can be fun, powerful, distracting, and dangerous. Your newly acquired knowledge will help tame the tech tigers in your daughter's life.

9

Teen Girl Social and Emotional Evolution

We human beings are social animals. Feeling loved, accepted, and understood impacts everything from physical resilience to mental functioning and emotional well-being. As you know, teen girls are relationship enthusiasts. During their teen years, they naturally turn toward peers like sunflowers following the sun. It's among their friends that they reveal and evolve aspects of their developing identities. Friendships knit girls into a sense of emotional community that comforts them and offers them a sense of place in the world.

However, friendships can also be very stressful for teen girls. They manage—for themselves and their friends—emotional states such as moodiness, social anxiety, insecurity, and self-consciousness. Often they hide these feelings because they feel pressured to please everyone and to be as perfect as possible. Given little support in learning ways to directly and skillfully communicate authentic thoughts and feelings, teen girls are unsure how to give feedback to friends and receive it from them. Read on to learn more about teen girl social and emotional development and how you can support your daughter.

You May Be Noticing:

○ She seems happiest when spending time with friends.

○ She demonstrates a growing ability to be a compassionate and committed friend.

○ Disruptions in friendships significantly affect her emotional state.

○ A social plan or invitation swiftly ignites her happiness, while exclusion from a social plan devastates her.

Then and Now: Teen Girl Social Development

When girls are very young, their social worlds are relatively simple and straightforward. They navigate social adventures zealously and have a disarmingly direct style of communication with peers: "Hey, Madison, you can go home now 'cause I'm done playing." Able to advocate for their own wants and needs, little girls easily provide emotional feedback for a partner in play: "Cody! That hurt my feelings! Don't ever, ever, say that again!" Disputes, often managed with adults nearby, are quickly resolved and forgotten. Because social dynamics are obvious and unsophisticated, parents have a sense of how their little girls are coming along socially.

When girls enter middle school, social development undergoes a surge of emotional intensification. The concept of "social power" makes a rude entrance into young teen awareness, and girls look around to see who has it and who doesn't. They start assessing which factors create acceptance or popularity and how they "measure up." With all developmental systems undergoing rapid transformation, peer acceptance appears to dangle an entrance sign to the land of milk and honey. In the minds of young teens, peer acceptance equals social success, and social success means "Phew! I must be okay!"

Social evolution is not easy for teen girls. The pendulum swings dramatically from a preteen "the world is my oyster" attitude toward life to a "please like and accept me" mentality. For many, the sudden fear that they may not be "okay," by new standards of okay-ness, is downright traumatizing. In an attempt to fit in and be accepted, teen girls may spend a lot of time thinking about appearance, acceptance, and popularity. Many, especially early bloomers, think a lot about boys and how to win their attention, and may be referred to as "boy crazy" by their parents.

Since obsessive thinking is common at this age, teen girls often admit they think a lot about perceived physical flaws (which they fear will threaten their acceptability) and the nuance of social interactions. Parents become anxious too because girls often talk more about their frustrations and anxieties than what's going well. Parents consult with professionals more during this transition than at many other times because (a) they want to know if their daughter's social focus and related emotional turmoil is "normal," and (b) they want to know how to ease the unrest.

> In the minds of young teens, peer acceptance equals social success, and social success means *"Phew! I must be okay!"*

To be emotionally attuned to your daughter while she is in her early teen years, remember that every day her mission is to

- avoid calling negative attention to herself;

- look as good as possible, by whatever standard is revered by her social group; and

- avoid making anyone angry, *especially anyone with social power.*

Because she's new to being a teen, she really wants to feel acceptable, and she looks to her social life to provide that feedback or reassurance.

Some teen girls attempt to decrease social stress by exiting mainstream expectations. Instead of trying to fit in, a teen may decide to circumvent that pressure by embracing or depicting herself as alternative. Taking this road less traveled is a way for some girls to maintain integrity to their authentic nature, while for others, it represents the exploration or the adoption of an identity designed as a defense against rejection. Often feisty kids use this strategy to get through the teen years with a sense of individuality (real or constructed) intact.

Regardless of strategy, over time teen girls become more comfortable with who they are and develop more confidence when relating to others. As their identity development unfolds, their emotions stabilize and their social development becomes more comfortable. This is especially true when girls have many ways to feel good about themselves, such as with meaningful activities, family relationships, good self-care, and varied interests.

Girls who are socially and emotionally observant find their flow quickly because they pay attention to what works socially and what doesn't. For example, they notice that girls who seek a lot of attention often become targets and are labeled "annoying" or worse, so they keep their own placement on the social radar lower. Other teen girls have a harder time reading social cues and cultivating an identity that flows with the social current, which makes their social development more painful.

Sound oppressive? It is, which is why college can be so wonderful. In college, the pendulum swings the other way and young adults are encouraged to be more expressive, creative, and original. College is often a time of reclaiming and expanding unique identity.

> Many healthy, well-adjusted teens experience a phase of confusion and scrambled identity, which they successfully move through before reclaiming treasured aspects of their authentic selves.

What It's Like for Parents

Parents share a sense of loss as they observe their previously vivacious and confident daughters strive to become more marketable versions of themselves. They see girls who expressed their thoughts and individuality easily at younger ages now afraid to do so for fear of social rejection. They observe girls who used to move, speak, and interact naturally become self-conscious, self-critical, and self-questioning.

Some girls are quite expressive about their turmoil, while others keep their emotions inside. Because much of teen girl social interaction occurs beyond the parameters of adult supervision, parents feel they miss much of what provokes teen girl social/emotional distress. It may soothe you to know that many healthy, well-adjusted teens experience a phase of confusion and scrambled identity, which they successfully move through before reclaiming treasured aspects of their authentic selves. This often occurs after the first couple of years of high school, making junior and senior years a more confident time. Original thinkers reclaim their innovation, goofballs reclaim their sense of humor, and entrepreneurial types regain their passion for moving and shaking. Of course, their identities evolve and become more mature and complex, but recognizable hallmarks of their younger selves are salvaged and reintegrated.

From Caretaking to Collaboration

With your teen daughter's expanding social appetite, it's a good time to expand her role as collaborator in making fun things happen. Girls need real-world skills, so have your daughter identify what needs to be done to make a social plan happen—and give her a role. For example, if she wants to bring three friends home from soccer practice, go to a movie, and then come back to your house for an overnight, have her identify the details that need attention, such as appropriate movie choice, theater location, and starting times, and then involve you for necessary support, such as drop-off and pick-up times. Teen girls can also plan meals together, cook, and clean up as part of their social time.

When you exchange caretaking for collaboration, you hand your daughter more responsibility and power over her life. Not only will she gain a sense of independence, mastery, and self-confidence, she will also learn to appreciate you as more than her facilitator. At this point in her life, it is useful for your daughter to see you as not only a major support but also as a person in your own right. When making social plans, let her know what you need to create a win-win situation for both of you. If you're cleaning up her huge mess in the kitchen, for example, you'll become understandably resentful. To avoid this, use the opportunity to bring your daughter into a larger, collaborative reality about healthy, mutually considerate relationships: "Andrea, I'm glad your friends are coming over. Please be 100 percent accountable for the messes you make. It's my weekend too and, like you, I need to balance the hard work I do with rest and fun. Thanks."

The alternative to a collaborative, give-and-take model of relationship is a one-direction model where teen girls expect their parents to facilitate their needs without contributing themselves. This is not good for teens or parents. Many parents complain that teen daughters are demanding or behave as if they are entitled to whatever they want—without realizing that, as parents, they have unintentionally created or allowed that model of relationship to flourish.

It's optimal when your daughter understands you have a lot to give, because you understand her needs and are committed to supporting her. At the same time, it's important that she understand that she is also a contributor to the family. When teen girls are exempt from clearing their dishes, feeding the dog, running an occasional errand *for you*, they naturally assume their role in the family is to receive without needing to contribute.

It's very natural for teen girls to be self-focused. In order for them to perceive and honor your needs and the needs of healthy family functioning, articulate that your daughter is expected to be a valuable family collaborator. These principles of give-and-take, mutuality, and reciprocity help teen girls develop relationship values to take into adulthood.

Before you can communicate your needs to your daughter, you must be clear about them yourself. Here's what some parents say they need:

o Girls to be quiet as a mouse by designated time; lights out by designated time.

o Requests to be asked in private. No putting parents "on the spot" in front of others.

o No leaving the house after a designated hour.

o Respect for younger siblings when friends are over.

o Chores finished by _____ (time).

Every parent—and family—will have different needs. Often those needs change over time. What doesn't change is the necessity of articulating those needs clearly.

Exercise: What Are Your Needs?

Think about your needs—quiet hours, language guidelines, household support, boundaries around borrowing, and so on. List them below and discuss them with your daughter.

_____

_____

_____

How You Can Ease Overthinking

As noted earlier, teen emotional and social development can trigger turmoil for girls who suffer bouts of "overthinking" about being accepted and acceptable. Although all people are susceptible to overthinking (also known as "obsessing" or "ruminating"), young teen girls are especially vulnerable. While some girls have a "water off a duck's back" mentality, other girls seek understanding and mastery through excessive mental review. They evaluate themselves, others, or the nuance of an interaction: *What did she mean by that? Did I act okay? Do I look okay? What should I wear? Did I embarrass myself?* Overthinking is a coping strategy run amok, because thinking is not a case of *more* being *better*. Learning to redirect stuck thoughts can help girls stabilize their moods and emotions.

In therapy, teen girls readily talk about overthinking. They are relieved to have the concept identified and discussed because it makes them feel less whacky about getting caught in it. Assessment of social interactions, sports or academic performance, and appearance are all common fodder for teen girl overthinking and can produce repetitive negative thoughts that harden into beliefs. I often help teen girls revise and move beyond "sticky" negative thoughts by writing new thoughts on bright index cards, which the teen can take home and read when she feels stuck. New thoughts are more positive, yet they must also be somewhat believable to the teen or she will disregard them. For one teen girl who overthought her appearance and believed her face was *"hideous,"* the new thought *My face is perfectly fine* was a believable replacement that made her feel better.

Exercise: Creating Positive Thoughts

Discuss the concept of overthinking with your daughter. Ask her if she has any negative thoughts that play over and over in her mind. Talk about how these thoughts can erode her self-confidence. Help your daughter make a list of these thoughts (like *I suck at math*) and create positive replacements (like *Math is challenging for me*):

Negative thoughts: **Positive Replacement Thoughts:**

_____   _____

_____   _____

_____   _____

_____   _____

When discussing overthinking, here are some concepts to consider and share:

It's really common. Many people just plain think too much! People who do it know it doesn't feel good. You can name the habit by asking something like "Honey, do you ever feel that you overthink things? Do you think so much that you feel stuck, that you're driving yourself crazy, or that you're making yourself feel worse?" Then tell her that overthinking is really common, we all do it sometimes, and we can change the habit. Instead of thoughts being in charge of your daughter, your daughter can be in charge of her thoughts.

Negative thoughts distort reality. Let her know that many people overthink because they feel that something productive will come of it, but that's not true! When people think too much, especially while in a not-so-great mood, thoughts become distorted.

Bad moods produce a perceptual bias that means all things yucky are blown up while other elements are ignored. If your daughter wants to think well about something, she needs to take a break from overthinking, take care of herself by doing something that helps her feel better, and revisit (or not!) the issue later.

When you find yourself overthinking, shift gears. Overthinking creates intense activation in emotional regions of the teen brain. These regions "cool down" once the teen switches gears, allowing emotions to restabilize. Here's what teen girls share about ways they shift gears:

○ My mom got me a progressive relaxation meditation CD that I listen to while lying on my bed. It helps me when I'm obsessing about social stuff or what I hate about myself. It really does work, even though I fought it at first. For me, I need help not thinking about things. Later those thoughts don't feel as upsetting or even true to me!

○ I've learned to write down my obsessive thoughts. Then I read them and realize they aren't that big of a deal. Sometimes I read them and they seem utterly ridiculous, so writing and reading gives me perspective. Sometime I crumple them up and throw them away, and it makes me feel better. My dad let me put them in the fireplace once, which was very satisfying.

○ When I get stuck on thoughts of the day, I tell a friend or my mom or my granny. They help me figure out what I can let go of and forget about and what I should handle. If I need to handle a social problem, they help me think of what I can do. Having a plan makes me feel better so I can move on!

○ When I overthink, I need to distract myself. I like watching TV, but my parents usually limit that, which means I do something like read a good book or draw or knit or sew. Distractions save me.

Exercise: Gear-Shifting Ideas

Discuss with your daughter ways she can switch gears when she finds herself over-thinking. List those ideas here:

_____

_____

_____

Meditation CDs

Teen girls are great candidates for listening to meditation CDs, so their minds can follow the voice and lead of the speaker. Meditation allows overthinking to cool, enhancing feelings of relaxation and well-being!

Assertiveness Practice

Sometimes your daughter will need to address a problem or social issue. If she decides to do this through personal communication, help her generate ideas and practice assertive dialogue with you. Remember, teen girls feel a lot of social pressure to please and "be nice," so teaching your daughter to skillfully communicate with her peers, teachers, and coaches is extremely helpful and empowering. Here's how a real-life conversation unfolded for one middle school girl and her mom:

Daughter: I can't stop thinking about how mean Shelley is. She called me fat today and it's all I can think about. Maybe I am fat!

Mom: *(supporting ventilation)* Tell me about it.

Daughter: *(shows face)* She said I looked like a fat chipmunk when I made this face at her.

Mom: *(reflecting and validating feelings while also identifying potential for resolution and communication)* No one likes the word "fat," even though she was probably referring to the silly face you were making. Did you tell her you didn't like her comment?

Daughter: Uhhh, not really, 'cause she would just say she's joking.

Mom: *(validating again followed by support planning future communication)* Maybe she is joking, but it's not funny to you. If she makes a comment like that again, is there something you'd want to say to give her feedback about how her words affect you?

Daughter: I feel like telling her that "fat" is a word she should never use—just because she's a beanpole, and not everyone is, and feelings can get hurt.

Mom: *(facilitating skillful wording to maximize successful communication)* That sounds good. You might want to start by saying, "I'm sure you don't mean to hurtful, but…" because that gives her the benefit of the doubt and will help her actually hear your feedback without getting defensive. I know I'm always more open to feedback when people start by saying something that makes me feel like they're giving me the benefit of the doubt, instead of assuming the worst about me. You know what I mean?

Daughter: Yeah, I do. I'll try that, and I'll leave the beanpole part out 'cause that will just cause more of a fight. Okay, Mom, I'm done talking about this.

Mom: *(accepting the cue)* Got it. If you feel like it, let me know how that goes.

In this example, overthinking about an interaction transitioned into an opportunity to practice skillful communication. The parent supported ventilation but also helped the daughter switch gears by creating a plan for "next time." Once your daughter understands the concept of overthinking, she may come to you for support saying, "I'm overthinking again." This is great because it shows she's integrating emotional intelligence vocabulary into her self-awareness.

More on Emotional Support

Regular reassurance is the bread and butter of supporting teen girls through social and emotional turbulence. Not only are they dealing with their own changeable moods, they're also navigating the moods of their friends, learning to deal with being "flaked on," coping with failed social plans, weathering the pain of being left out or forgotten, and learning to get along with many different personalities. Add romantic relationships to that lineup and you have emotional overstimulation.

Never underestimate the impact your reassuring words have on her.

As you help your teen daughter through this time of emotional turbulence, never underestimate the impact your reassuring words have on her. Even when she doesn't completely believe your words, your devotion to comforting her finds its mark. Slip in short and sweet reassurances that (a) you understand and support her, and that (b) her feelings are valid and normal, as are the challenges provoking them. Here are a few examples of reassuring statements:

○ I really understand how intense social stuff is at this age. It's very normal and I promise it gets easier.

○ It's natural to feel really affected by social ups and downs. You can always talk to me and I'll be a great listener.

○ I remember how hard it is to make plans when you're a teen! It's frustrating, and so much seems to go wrong or fall apart. It gets much better when you're older.

○ You can talk through your feelings with me, and I won't judge you or any of your friends harshly. I remember how frustrating social stuff was as a teenager.

○ Honey, it's hard being your age. There's a lot going on and it's just hard. I get it.

Statements like this give your daughter a little oasis of emotional attunement from someone she can trust to have her back. It also reinforces your bond, which creates a bouquet of benefits for a stressed teen girl.

Avoid Teasing

Parents, often dads, tease as a way to make a connection or as a way to respond to teen girl social turmoil. Dads often say their intentions are to lighten the mood, cheer things up, or create perspective. Teasing is risky, because instead of lightening a teen girl's mood, she may feel invalidated, exposed, or humiliated. Even if the teasing is well intended, it may cause hurt feelings and withdrawal. Teasing creates an emotional atmosphere that is unsafe.

Warning: Especially do not tease teen girls by sexualizing or romanticizing their relationships with the opposite sex—or the same sex. Teen girls need to be able to have nonsexual relationships with both sexes without someone poking fun at them. If your daughter has siblings who indulge in this kind of teasing, express a very clear and strong message that such teasing is unacceptable. If there is a romantic component involved, it's even more important to protect teen girls from teasing.

High-Talk vs. Low-Talk Girls

Parenting a teen girl can be challenging. However, if you have a talking teen who tells you a lot about her social life, you're less confused. You know which friends she loves lately and which ones annoy her. You know who she thinks is cool and maybe whom she has a crush on or a relationship with. You have access to support her, comfort her, and socially guide her.

For example, if she's in a quandary about whether or not to tell Beth that Carrie was flirting with Chris, you can share your life experience and thoughts about potential risks and benefits. If she feels resentful toward her b.f.f. for spending their overnight texting a love interest, you can help your daughter practice ways of speaking up that are assertive and skillful. If she's an overthinker and downloading interactions from her day, you can support her by listening to her vent and then reminding her to switch gears to avoid getting stuck on negative thoughts. When teens discuss what's going on in their social lives, parents have clearer access to providing useful support.

More likely and more challenging, you have a low-talk teen or a hit-and-miss talker. She may share on a need-to-know basis and feel you need to know very little. She may be less verbally communicative by nature, or she may just be telling you less as part of her separation process. If your daughter doesn't share details about her social life, you rely on your own observations. You know who she's bringing home and, at least sometimes, with whom she's hanging out. You know what activities and affiliations she has and may have a sense of which friends and acquaintances accompany which activities.

With a low-talk teen, you also rely on how your daughter appears to you. If she seems to be a satisfied social animal, you're probably staying aware without needing to get too involved. If she spends a lot of time alone in her room or is tearful or irritable, you may suspect an upset in a friendship, exclusion from something, or an overall lack of social connection, and you may be frustrated that your daughter isn't sharing her struggles with you.

Special Considerations for Low-Talk Teens

If and when your low-talk teen tests you by sharing a scrap of her personal life, let the conversation remain hers; don't overwhelm her with your thoughts, feelings, and suggestions. If you're a high-talk parent, think about decreasing your verbal activity by 90 percent; this allows your daughter to be the "alpha" while you receive her thoughts and feelings. Low-talk teen girls often need more time and space in a conversation to identify their feelings and verbalize them, so high-talk parents need to be very careful not to take over the conversation.

Low-talk teens sometimes work through their feelings in low-talk ways. They may engage in other activities such as dance, theater, or art, all of which help teen girls express themselves. Journaling is fabulous for low-talk teens who use their journals to move through feelings. Some teens get really creative and make their journals artistic, which is a wonderful way to vent big feelings. Journals come in many sizes and designs, so taking your daughter to pick one out is a sweet way of connecting and showing support. Let your daughter know her journal is private, that you will never read it, and stick to that promise.

Danger sign: Some teens don't talk even when they are experiencing huge social problems. If your daughter resists going to school, has trouble concentrating or doing her schoolwork, or seems sad, anxious, withdrawn, or upset, she may be the victim, participant, or bystander in bullying.

What Is Teen Girl Bullying?

As mentioned earlier, girls in our culture are expected to be nice, good at everything, and liked by everyone. Because our culture has trouble accepting and supporting girls in being displeasing, they're left to hide or deny many of their uncomfortable, angry, and aggressive feelings. While a sad girl often gets a hug, angry girls are sent to their rooms or called "bitches." They are often not taught skills that can facilitate productive communication and resolution to inevitable social conflicts. Of course, hidden and denied feelings don't just disappear; they may morph into behaviors our culture increasingly recognizes as girl bullying.

In the book *Odd Girl Out*, Rachel Simmons (2002) brought the distinct nature of *girl bullying* (also called "relational aggression" or "alternate aggression") to public attention. No longer are stereotypes of bullying confined to being pushed in hallways or slammed against lockers. More and more, whispering, spreading rumors, and being excluded are recognized as ways girls use aggression where it really hurts: in the context of relationships. Unlike general bullying where nonmainstream kids are disproportionately targeted, anything can make a teen girl a target of bullying. No one's exempt.

With technology serving as a huge forum for teen communication, acts of bullying are as easy as making a mean comment on someone's "wall," spurring a dog-pile effect in which dozens more people add to the initial comment, effectively eviscerating the target. Ugh! The warp-speed evolution of technology far outpaces efforts to control how it's used. Cases of teens committing suicide after being bullied have brought all forms of bullying to public attention. The educational system invests big money into antibullying campaigns, and most states now have laws against it.

To keep perspective, remember that a great deal of bullying behavior occurs because teen girls naturally experience huge lapses in judgment, sensitivity, and social intelligence. Behavior that appears vicious is often caused by obliviousness, self-absorption, confusion, and misunderstanding. Especially when girls are in their young teen years, social "mistakes" are made because teen girls really, truly, do not realize how other people experience their comments and behavior. Stuck in what it's like to be themselves, girls can completely fail to put themselves in the shoes of another. In other words, cluelessness is often the root of teen girl insensitivity, a developmental glitch that improves over time! Here are points to keep in mind regarding teen girl bullying:

> Most of the behavior that causes social-emotional pain for teen girls is unintentional.

Name the issue of girl bullying. Girls are more likely to open up to adults they feel have a clue about what's going on in their lives. Your daughter needs to know that you are familiar with information on girl bullying. Share what you know and clarify that girls can be involved as bullies, bystanders, or victims. Invite her to tell you what she knows about it, or what she's experienced. Let her know that you will support her if she feels she has bullied, stood by while another girl was bullied, or been the victim of a bully. Consult *Odd Girl Out* by Rachel Simmons for excellent questions you can ask your daughter to get a conversation going.

Respect starts at home. The more children are treated with respect and held accountable for treating others with respect at home, the more they recognize behavior that deviates from a respectful standard. Keeping a loving, intellectually stimulating home environment and spending time with teens reduces involvement in bullying.

Talk to school administrators. Some schools are becoming savvy and responsive to the issue of girl bullying. See if your daughter's school provides education and support for bullying. Encourage awareness and advocate for an antibullying curriculum.

Monitor screen time. Girl communication can be a runaway train on social networking sites. Your daughter may be committing acts of bullying without being aware she has crossed a line. She may be a bystander observing hurtful communication. Or she may be getting bullied but not want to tell you for fear of parental involvement. Regularly check out her online activities. Expand her awareness about the different forms of bullying and the potentially devastating effects.

Teach emotional intelligence. Talk about what you do with your strong feelings. Talk about skillful and unskillful ways people handle their emotions. Anger is not a bad feeling, and we are wired as humans to have it. It has evolutionary value. What people do with their anger can be hurtful and cruel, or it can be empowered and skillful. Blaming and raging at others is unskillful and may shade into bullying. Talking about feelings in your home as well as the many choices people can make in response to their feelings improves emotional intelligence.

More Ideas to Support Your Daughter Socially

You play an important role in your daughter's social and emotional development. Here are a few ways to turn your love and support into concrete action:

Create a teen-friendly environment. Since she wants to spend a lot of her time with friends, it might as well be at your house! That way you're in the loop regarding who is important to her, and you know she is in a safe, supervised environment. Here are some ideas:

- Get to know the key players in her social life. Know their names and greet them when they enter your home.

- Create a teen-friendly place for your girl to hang out. Beanbag chairs, floor pillows, and soft blankets are big hits. Interactive computer games, pool tables, Ping-Pong, and board games create fun ways for teens to interact.

- Facilitate movie rentals and provide snacks.

- Make a habit of circulating through areas where teens collect without being one of them. Your occasional presence (not intrusion) will keep everyone on best behavior.

- Cultivate relationships with parents of your daughter's friends. Stay connected.

- When boys are involved, be unapologetic about stating house rules: "Hey guys, we've got plenty of food, so help yourselves and clean up when you're done. The door stays open and pickup is at 11 o'clock."

Join with other families: Many teens prefer hanging with their families when dynamics are enriched by the presence of other people. Kids and parents are naturally at their best during group activities. Multifamily dinners, vacations, and outings go a long way in building good feelings. These group activities may work for you:

- Rotate dinners with a few other families. Make-your-own burritos or pizzas can be fun and easy. Teens can contribute by coming up with ideas for food and fun.

- Meet other families for a day of activity (hiking, bowling, fishing, or kayaking). Let the teens plan some part of it.

- Organize multifamily camping trips. Each family plans designated meals. Let the kids create a skit that pokes fun at parents or whatever theme entertains them.

- Host a multifamily tradition such as scary movies every Friday the 13th, full-moon bonfires with s'mores, block parties, and garage sales. The possibilities are endless!

Save her place. As your daughter experiments with more "socially acceptable" versions of herself, hold the truth of all her deep identity qualities inside your mind and heart. If she was a funny, thoughtful little girl with a big heart for stray animals, remember those qualities. She will likely reclaim them when she's less socially distracted.

Help her diversify. If your daughter seems underconnected or is changing friend groups, look for activities where she can form new friendships. If school friends are getting her down, she may feel better spending time with established family friends or family. She may be open to beginning a new activity with a fresh group of kids. Sometimes teen girls feel energized when they work with young kids or the elderly. Look for fresh connections.

Be available. Many teen girls report spending hours and hours alone. If girls are having a hard time socially because they are underconnected, changing friends, outgrowing friends, or experiencing conflict, it's a great time to have you around. Your daughter may want more time with you or may just feel comforted to have you in the house with her. Girls who go through hard social times strongly benefit from a good relationship with at least one parent. They don't necessarily want to have long, deep talks about what's going on socially, but they often like the feeling of having a parent who loves them close by.

Let her hone her relationship skills with you. Teen girls are working on important skills such as speaking up for themselves, asking for what they want and need from people, articulating limits for how they want to be treated, and more. It's a really good time to notice your daughter practicing these skills in the family and with you. Instead of getting angry and quashing her pluck, when she stands up to you, applaud her assertiveness while letting her know when she's crossing a respect line. Even if you don't say yes to her request, affirm her growing communication skills whenever you can.

Late social bloomers. Family connectedness is more crucial for late social bloomers. If your daughter doesn't belong to a group of friends, you, your family, and close family friends may be her primary social group. Know that you serve a very important purpose, and keep a creative eye out for ways to gently and slowly expand her social opportunities.

At this point in your reading, you've learned a lot about teen girl development and ways you can support your daughter. The next and final chapter on happiness will help you enjoy your daughter and your life more fully.

10

Cultivating Happiness

If you ask a parent what they really, really want for their teen daughter, most will say, "I want her to be happy!" Even parents who drive their daughters to achieve believe that achievement leads to success and success leads to happiness. Embedded in the phrase "leads to happiness" is a belief that happiness is an endpoint, a pot-of-gold reward attained once achievements and goals are realized. This strategy overlooks an important truth: if you're not happy during the journey, you won't suddenly be happy at the destination.

> If you're not happy during the journey, you won't suddenly be happy at the destination.

But what is happiness exactly? *Happiness* is a state characterized by the experience of positive emotions and a sense of meaning. Because happiness is a state of mind and not an endpoint, if we don't learn to cultivate it along the way, we may fall apart en route or be too burned out to flourish once we get there. With high levels of stress accepted as the new normal, teens and parents alike often live for the hope that somehow things will get better in the future.

You May Be Noticing:

o Happiness seems like a fuzzy concept, more idealistic than realistic.

o You (and your daughter) expend more energy getting things done than cultivating happiness—or you (and your daughter) are not expending *enough* energy getting things done, so you don't feel in control of your life or your happiness.

o The notion of actively cultivating happiness seems self-indulgent, hedonistic, shallow, or immature.

What's the point of this chapter? Don't wait for the future! Expand your experience of happiness now.

The field of positive psychology has made the topic of happiness a hot area of research. Thanks to numerous studies, we know more about how to create and sustain happiness. Some results will surprise you, so read on to learn ways you can protect and expand happiness in your family.

Where Did All the Fun Go?

Didn't the fun of being a kid used to last longer than it has for our daughters? Parents sometimes worry that their daughters aren't experiencing enough happiness. Sure, they seem relatively peaceful when watching a movie, but do they experience enough joy, meaningful engagement, laughter, and fun? Or is their happiness and sense of meaning suffocated by too much stress and too many concerns, both personal and global? We had concerns when we were their age, but truly, their overall stresses seem higher because they are! Without knowing a better way, parents shrug their shoulders and believe that our world today is different and our girls just need to deal with it.

Instead of "supporting" teen girls to keep their heads down and push through, or beseeching them away from technology to engage with us or in other activities, we can reallocate that parenting energy in a way that just might surprise them. We can engage our family members in conversations about happiness. Since cultivating happiness energizes productivity, success, and well-being, it makes sense to tap into it each day. Rather than serving as a distraction to productivity, it can be the fuel. After all, expanding happiness can sometimes be as simple as doing what you already do but in a different way. Instead of gulping down your morning coffee while fretting about your day, you create a tiny niche of happiness by drinking it on your porch while petting your dog and mulling over a few things you feel grateful for. There are many, many ways to stoke your happiness, and partaking in a routine activity, with intentional enjoyment, is just one.

Delaying Gratification Too Long

Some teen girls, often labeled "lazy," are actually experiencing a state of confusion or "engagement paralysis." Disengaged teen girls aren't effectively tapped into their life force energy, which renders them minimally active, creative, and connected. Since screen time requires no physical, social, or intellectual commitment, disengaged girls passively soothe and entertain themselves as a way to numbly pass the day.

College-bound teen girls often look forward to their near future: freedom, fun, and fulfillment must equal happiness, right? Unfortunately it often doesn't work out this way. The years of enduring too much stress, sacrificing balanced development, and delaying gratification do not set them up for a happiness payoff. A nationwide survey of American colleges found that nearly 30 percent of college students reported feeling "so depressed that it was difficult to function" at some time in the past year (American College Health Association 2010).

While the above finding is disturbing, it makes sense when you consider the trend. If greater numbers of stressed-out, emotionally underdeveloped girls hobble out of high school to enter college, why would they suddenly flourish with a scene change? Without knowing how to nurture happiness and well-being, advancing to the next stage of life often results in a late-adolescent failure-to-thrive syndrome. Instead of mastering various challenges and relishing the joys of college, too many young women get sucked down into a rabbit hole of negative mood states and undeveloped coping strategies. No matter where your daughter falls on the "drive" spectrum, focusing on the cultivation of true happiness will plant seeds for healthy development.

Inside Happiness

Martin Seligman began a new era of psychology in 1998 when, as president of the American Psychological Association, he chose the study of happiness as the theme for his term. Collaborating with other leading psychologists, Seligman struck the match for an explosion of research on happiness that has produced a flurry of studies and books on the topic. Because happiness is a subjective experience, researchers have created simple self-report surveys to both identify and rate factors that do and do not affect it (Seligman 2002).

Happiness: Fact and Fiction

The study of happiness resulted in some interesting—and unexpected—findings. Some of the things we thought were true about happiness turned out to be false—and vice versa. Let's look at some of the findings that are most relevant to parenting our teen daughters.

FICTION: More Money = More Happiness. This is an important research finding, because our daughters grow up in an incredibly materialistic, fame-frenzied, money-crazed culture. Watch a little "reality" television and you'll see our culture's fascination with the ratings-grabbing trifecta: rich, hot, and misbehaving! For developing teen girls, repetitive cultural messages give the impression that money does indeed buy happiness.

In his book *Stumbling on Happiness*, researcher Dan Gilbert (2006) debunked the money-buys-happiness myth with his finding that, although money makes a big difference when people are so poor they can't meet basic needs, it fails to bring greater happiness past that point. In other words, rich people are no happier than people who have less money. Human beings quickly adapt to the happiness produced by new luxuries that money buys, thus neutralizing the initial thrill.

FACT: Higher Incomes + Material Goodies ≠ Happiness. If higher incomes and material goodies don't make people happy, what does? Job satisfaction and good social networks do. Enjoying your work and feeling connected to people increase happiness.

Gilbert therefore encourages people to pursue work they enjoy and to actively nurture social relationships.

During a car ride or over dinner, initiate a conversation and ask your family members to talk about their personal definition of happiness. Accept and appreciate all answers. You may expand to talking about what makes them feel happy, or when and with whom they feel the happiest. If your family enjoys the conversation, ask them to name their top five happiest memories. Even recalling and talking about happiness helps people feel happier, so this exercise has many benefits: it introduces the topic as worthy of attention; it gets people talking, thinking, and remembering; it serves as a springboard from which you can launch further conversations on the value of happiness.

Choosing Happiness

Some people feel squeamish about considering their own happiness in choice making and life planning, believing to do so would be frivolous or shallow. Instead of feeling squeamish, you're much better off regarding happiness as a big, fat, juicy pie to take bites from. Taking bites (and enjoying them!) creates positive ripples everywhere you go, with everyone you meet, and in everything you do. Figuring out how to live your life in order to maximize your happiness is a gift to everyone, so by all means choose happiness!

Happiness and Meaningful Work

Remember connecting the dots from chapter 5? We can use it again here as a way to connect the concepts of work and job satisfaction, since the combo stokes happiness levels. When your daughter talks about the work world, weave in questions or comments that connect the importance of personal satisfaction to work. Although it's wise to avoid saying something negative about one of her interests, you can facilitate further investigation on her part or collaborate with her on gathering more information. (Oftentimes girls will eliminate ideas on their own, and it's best for them to do that without parental input.) For example, one father felt concerned by his daughter's interest in the military. Instead of communicating his concerns, he jumped online with her to learn more about her interests.

You can also connect the dots by verbally "noticing" a person who exemplifies job satisfaction: "Reilly, isn't it cool the way some people just love their work and you can tell?" Sometimes you can even strike up conversations with people about their work and how they feel about it. Look for opportunities to connect the dots with your daughter to (a) plant seeds about the importance of work satisfaction, (b) elicit her thoughts, ideas, and observations; and (c) energize further exploration. Again, you're letting her know that the consideration of happiness is valid and valuable, because you're focusing your attention on the pairing of happiness and work.

> People create what they *want* in life by identifying and releasing what they don't want.

We can tell our girls that, even though they won't be happy every moment, they can and should consciously make choices that nourish happiness. Since work takes up a lot of adult life, our daughters will be happier if they pursue work they enjoy and that has meaning for them. Of course, since they're discovering their gifts, talents, and interests, they're often unsure of their career path. One parent shares her story of receiving encouragement to pursue meaningful work:

> I'll never forget my high school English teacher who asked me why I wanted to be a lawyer. I said, "To make lots of money and get respect from other people." He told me to seriously reconsider my choice, based on the reasons I gave him. He asked me what I would really love to do if my highest priorities were neither prestige nor money. I'd never deeply considered what I'd love to do, and no one had ever asked me. I changed my course to eventually pursue a field deeply interesting and meaningful to me. To this day, I have never had a moment of dreading my work. Sure, I'd like more vacation time and more money, but I love what I do and it's a very good fit for who I am. I let my kids know they must pursue work that they love.

We can support our teen girls as they identify what they do and don't find interesting by helping them talk through their impressions, questions, and concerns. For example, I've heard many teen girls say they'd love to pursue psychology but fear it would make them too sad. Such comments give me an opportunity to share how fulfilling I find my work. I let girls know that I've cultivated beliefs and habits that support me in feeling quite happy and grateful most of the time. While I feel compassion for clients going through hard times, I don't take on the emotions of other people and suffer because of them. Not only would that be painful and exhausting, it would impair my ability to be helpful. I also share different work opportunities in the field of psychology, as well as details regarding educational paths. Teen girls need to talk to lots of different adults in lots of different careers so they can get a spectrum of feedback. Think about how you can support this process. Sometimes we need to reassure teen girls that all work-related exploration is positive, even if girls ultimately reject further investigation. One of the ways people create what they *want* in life is by identifying and releasing what they don't want. Teen girls benefit from support exploring, experiencing, examining, and refining their interests in order to pursue work they enjoy.

Exercise: Exploring Interests

Approach your daughter for a quick and fun brainstorming session to get her thinking about work she would enjoy. Working together, make a list of her strengths, interests, and gifts. One mother and daughter wrote, "Jessie is a people person, an extrovert; she's happiest around groups of people. She has high energy, is a good communicator and strategic thinker, and is calm under pressure. She likes to talk and negotiate."

My Strengths

_____

My Interests

_____

My Gifts

_____

Discuss jobs and professions where she might use her strengths, interests, and gifts. Jessie and her mom wrote, "Jessie would like to be in charge of people and projects. She is attracted to the idea of a business setting and managing a product or service she finds interesting." Welcome all ideas and list them below:

Possible Jobs and Professions

_____

_____

_____

Are there any fields of work that your daughter wants to know more about? If so, what are they? Jessie listed the following: hotel management, advertising, marketing or public relations; some kind of job where you launch products; some kind of business where you organize different groups toward a goal.

Fields of Work I Want to Explore

_____

_____

_____

In considering the information above, what resources can your daughter consult to gain more practical information? Resources might include friends or relatives who work in different fields, vocational counselors, job fairs, or written materials.

Resources to Check Out

_____

_____

_____

Teen girls benefit from fun-ish, light-ish discussions that help them feel hopeful and positive about their futures. Connecting the concept of future work to her strengths, interests, and gifts puts her on the right trajectory.

Happiness and Relationships

Along with job satisfaction, good social relationships boost happiness. Although you just learned about teen girl social relationships in chapter 9, you can also improve your daughter's relationship skills in the context of the relationship she has with you. Since pointing out the good is always more effective than focusing on the bad, help her form her solid social identity by offering feedback about what you see and experience. For instance, "You know, Beth, you were so calm and helpful when I couldn't find my keys this morning. It really meant a lot to me. I bet you're that way with friends too." Beth was in the mood to engage with her dad and shared a few examples of how she offered calm support to her friends. Help teen girls appreciate their social strengths, which in turn helps them build a solid social identity and self-confidence.

Some girls need support in building friendship skills. Common teen girl social complaints include girls who talk only about themselves, girls who are competitive and "one-up" other girls, poor listening skills, and expressing too much negativity. One mom noticed her daughter's habit of interrupting teen friends yet failing to register their annoyance. She felt it would be most productive if she waited until her daughter displayed the same behavior with her so she could compassionately bring the habit to her daughter's attention: "I know you don't realize it, honey, but you just interrupted me. It's really frustrating for me, even though I know you don't mean to be rude."

This conversation was successful in large part because this mom shared that she too struggled with interrupting, but worked on it so that she could improve her relationships. While the feedback stung the teen for a moment, her mom's skillful self-disclosure and kind approach helped the teen accept and utilize the feedback. Mom and daughter even created a strategy to address the habit, which involved the daughter repeating the words *patient and relaxed listening* in her head while her friends talked. Within one week, the teen reported improved interactions with friends and a sense of pride in her ability to change.

For strong social functioning, encourage girls to smile, show warmth and friendliness, express interest, offer encouragement, and respect boundaries. I tell teen girls that everyone wants the same thing socially: to know that they're safe! People who smile and show friendliness make other people feel at ease; they feel emotionally safe.

> Everyone wants the same thing socially: to know that they're safe!

When teen girls feel a level of trust with others, they can begin to share more personal information about themselves. To maintain good, healthy boundaries, girls should not share personal information that makes them feel too exposed or emotionally unsafe.

Teen girls who want more social connection get a lot of mileage out of ramping up the eye contact–smile combo. I suggest teen girls experiment with "a fake it till you make it" day in which they exude warmth and confidence all day. To exude confidence, they must commit to accessing a sense of belief and trust in themselves, which they convey through eye contact, smiling, walking and interacting with pride, and making contact with others. A friendly gesture can be as simple as saying, "Hey, how's it goin'?" to the person sitting at the next desk in biology. The results that come from this experiment create a sense of power along with positive social momentum that can significantly improve a day—both hers and someone else's.

Even if your daughter rolls her eyes when you remind her to greet the neighbors on the way into the house, she stills hears you. The more positively you phrase the reminder, the better she'll take it in: "Hey, Michaela, don't forget to take a few moments to acknowledge the neighbors. Your smile makes a difference to people."

One reason teen girls love therapy is that they get to learn more about themselves. Oftentimes when I reflect something about a girl, I am charmed by her response of surprise and delight. For instance, I may comment that she shows an impressive ability to think flexibly about a situation. She beams and smiles, having had no previous appreciation for this strength. Absorbing the reflection allows her to expand her self-perception and appreciation of what she has to offer. Teen girls need caring adults in their lives for many reasons, positive reflecting being one.

Exercise: Relationship Strengths

Together, discuss and write down your teen's relationship strengths. For example, Ava and her dad wrote, "Ava is very direct and authentic with her friends. She's sincere, and people feel that. She inspires trust, and her friends confide in her regularly. She's fun and spontaneous. She's not afraid to be goofy."

My Relationship Strengths

_____

_____

_____

Ask your daughter to consider social areas she might like to improve. Sometimes a route to this information is to ask if she ever gets feedback from her friends about things she might want to change. One daughter confided to her parent that friends had "called her out on" taking a joke too far, while another parent learned her daughter got feedback about "blowing off" social plans to be with her boyfriend.

Ava and her dad wrote, "Ava wants to be more open to new friends instead of limiting herself to her 'besties.' She wants to be more outgoing socially, which will be great practice for college."

Areas that I'd Like to Improve

_____

_____

_____

Now you and your daughter have a few items on your radar that you can support and nurture. Understanding the importance of work satisfaction and strong social networks helps you guide your daughter to authentic sources of happiness.

Creating More Happiness

Researcher Sonja Lyubomirsky asserts in her book *The How of Happiness* (2007) that while 50 percent of our happiness is determined by genetic setpoint, only 10 percent comes from life circumstances (money, beauty, marital status), leaving a full 40 percent available to play with and expand. She suggests we make the most of the 40 percent we control.

Developing positive habits such as exercise and meditation have a huge impact on happiness. Subtle but powerful practices such as practicing forgiveness and gratitude likewise increase happiness. Learning to be more present "in the moment" instead of overthinking about worries and concerns isn't always easy, but it definitely helps people tap into happiness. What do your family members have to say about habits, choices, or behaviors that increase happiness in their lives?

Introducing Flow

Flow refers to the state of well-being we experience when totally immersed in a pleasurable activity. While in the state of flow, we may lose track of time and experience blissful engagement with what we're doing. Here is how some parents describe their sense of flow:

- I'm a runner, which I've always thought of as my therapy, but maybe running is more accurately my flow activity. I get a break from thinking when I run, and it makes me feel fantastic.

- Gardening is my flow activity. Two hours can go by like ten minutes when I'm working in my garden.

- Playing music is a time when I'm most focused and happy. It's an altered state of consciousness that renews me.

Exercise: Increasing Flow

Discuss the concept of flow with your daughter. Help her identify her flow activities and list them below:

My Flow Activities

_____

_____

_____

How do these activities make me feel?

_____

_____

_____

A father of a thirteen-year-old client who had difficulty thinking of a single flow activity took her to an art store, where she picked out a calligraphy starter kit. She loved it and replaced some of her screen time with calligraphy time. For many teen girls, art, dance, playing a sport, or playing music provide a sense of flow. Ideally "flow" will become a regular part of your teen girl's schedule.

Happiness-expanding activities can be practiced both individually and/or as a family. One activity to consider is practicing gratitude.

Practicing Gratitude

Researchers Robert Emmons and M. E. McCullough (2003) brought the concept of gratitude to world attention, noting that when we focus on what we are grateful for, we expand happy feelings and radiate warmth to other aspects of our lives. If you work on this happiness expander, you are likely to find yourself savoring sweet moments in your life more fully.

Initiate a gratitude ritual at family dinner by sharing one or two things you're grateful for. Invite other family members to do the same. This ritual is great because everyone gets to hear a blurb about everyone else's day while also practicing focusing on the positive, which becomes a happiness habit. When everyone gets the hang of this, you may note more gratitude expressed beyond the dinner table too.

KEEPING A GRATITUDE JOURNAL

You may want to keep a gratitude journal in which you list things you are grateful for. When you express appreciation in this manner, you may notice your mind looking for things you will later record. This is a small but extremely powerful shift in thinking: you engage your mind to track, note, and record positive things. Since what we focus on creates how we feel, why not focus on things we're grateful for? You'll notice wonderful effects, including increased energy, improved relationships, improved mood, increased ability to forgive and feel empathy, and much more.

Teen girls often love keeping a personal gratitude journal. You can take your daughter to pick one out or provide materials to make one for herself.

Here are examples of what my teen clients have shared from their gratitude journals. Today I am grateful for

- my mom's key lime pie;

- my dad's patience teaching me to drive;

- sleeping in;

- my puppy's puppy-breath;

- my cozy bed and yellow comforter;

- my best friend's laugh.

Over time, practicing gratitude becomes part of your natural consciousness. Gratitude is both subtle and extremely powerful in that it involves teaching yourself to pay attention to, acknowledge, and luxuriate in the spectrum of sweet moments in your life.

Redefine "On Track"

If our culture emphasizes *"Be on track, stay on track"* for teens and their parents, we parents can make the cultivation of happiness part of "the track." As noted in chapter 7, teen girls can become so focused on staying on track with commitments that they sacrifice balance and well-being. The solution is not to abstain from activities and commitments. As parents, we simply need to make sure our girls are well suited for their commitments and activities, that our girls are committed because *they* truly want to be, and that their commitments are reasonable and yield an overall positive experience. We may need to step in when the choice or intensity of a commitment strangles the experience of joy and meaning. When the stress-to-happiness ratio is unfavorable, teen girls need our support in releasing commitments and choosing activities that generate more happiness.

Reviewing commitments and assessing the stress-to-happiness ratio helps protect your daughter both now and in the future. When you sit down with her to do the exercise below, you send a message about the importance of her happiness. Instead of feeling superficial or frivolous for seeking and protecting happiness in her life, she'll have a sense of healthy entitlement to create a life that honors happiness.

Exercise: On Track with Happiness

Step 1: Together with your daughter, list her activities and commitments. Then pause and get a sense of the list together.

Activity/Commitment	Stress Rating	Happiness Rating

Step 2: Using a scale of 1 to 10 (1 = very little stress; 10 = high stress), have your daughter rate the stress she experiences for each activity/commitment. Then pause so she can emotionally register the feelings that may surface.

Step 3: Using a scale of 1 to 10 (1 = low happiness; 10 = high happiness), have your daughter rate the happiness she experiences with each activity/commitment. (You may find that your daughter needs to define what happiness actually means to her.) Again, pause after this step so your daughter can look at her life from this perspective. Looking at things in this explicit manner helps girls to emotionally register and intellectually evaluate the quality and quantity of their activities.

Step 4: Ask her if there is anything she'd like to change about the list. Depending on the level of stress and unhappiness, commitments are sometimes broken in order to reestablish the teen's well-being. While difficult, preserving your daughter's health and well-being take precedence. Sometimes a commitment can be completed, but then a decision is made not to renew that commitment in the future.

More Ideas to Boost Happiness

You know how good begets good? Well, happiness begets more happiness! Keep your momentum going by integrating these ideas into your family's growing repertoire of happiness activities.

Prompt acts of thoughtfulness. Acts of kindness and consideration warm relationships like rays of golden sunshine. Because it's developmentally appropriate for teen girls to be quite consumed by their own lives, gently prompt your daughter toward acts of thoughtfulness: "Hey, Cara, have you checked in with Quinn to see if her strep throat is better? I remember how lonely you felt when you had mono. If you want, we can drop off a magazine or something for her."

Supply fun stokers. Look for opportunities to bring fun and play into your daughter's life. Play is a great de-stressor, and we all need to feel like kids again. Play-Doh, Silly Putty, bubbles, yo-yos, juggling, dress-up, face paint, water balloons, water guns, Smashball, or inexpensive toys she enjoyed at younger ages can, from time to time, appeal to your teen girl. Whether she's hanging out with her friends or with her family, fun stokers create an opportunity for a good laugh.

Manage your stress. In order to be happy, you and your daughter need good, solid ways of handling the stress. Having meltdowns feels horrible, upsets people, and gets us nowhere in our problem solving. Holding stress inside feels awful, creates depression and anxiety, and also gets us nowhere. Good, solid coping includes breathing through stressful moments, maintaining self-control over behavior and communication, taking time-outs when necessary, and creating solutions that can be executed one step at a time. If you are a high-stress person, get support through a stress management program or mindfulness-based stress reduction (MBSR) program in your area. See what's available.

Forgive and forget. When approached skillfully, working through conflict creates deeper bonds between people. When conflict arises between you and your daughter, apologize when appropriate (fully and generously), and forgive regularly (willingly and completely). Carrying the heavy weight of "earning back trust" shames teen girls and is nonbeneficial. Instead of burying her in the "bad," forgive her fully and articulate your expectation for future behavior with optimism and goodwill.

Savor the little things in life. When she sees how delighted you are by life's simple pleasures, your delight both gives her a sense of security and shows her the path of true happiness. A lottery winner is not happier than the mom enjoying a mango popsicle while relaxing in a plastic chair near the sprinkler on a hot day—or a dad who counts his blessings, which includes having a teen daughter who calls him "Daddy" when her friends aren't around.

Live in the present moment. In any given moment, most of us find we are truly okay. Sure, stressors and challenges swirl around us, but worrying about them doesn't change their outcome! Try being in the present moment (as opposed to stuck in thoughts about the future or the past) a little bit each day. This is called *mindfulness meditation*, and you can practice it while petting your dog or even doing the dishes. Bring your full attention to the present moment by slowing down and gently bending away from your five million thoughts to be in the present moment. Pay attention to your slow, even breathing or the expression on your dog's face as you pet her, or the color of the grass, or whatever your senses are experiencing. If you're soon pulled back into thoughts of the future or past, it's okay! That's why they call mindfulness a practice.

Congratulations on completing *Parenting a Teen Girl*! In the present moment, I feel **grateful** to be sharing this reading and writing experience with you. Like you, I will continue to bring my best efforts to parenting teen girls, knowing that some moments will be better than others. I hope the ideas and tips you've learned will support you in maximizing the good moments while comforting you through the challenges. Blessings to you and your daughter.

References

American College Health Association. *American College Health Association–National College Health Assessment II: Reference Group Data Report Fall 2010.* Linthicum, MD: American College Health Association, 2011. Accessed September 26, 2011. www.acha-ncha.org.

Associated Press–MTV Poll. 2007. *Youth Happiness Study.* Accessed June 22, 2010. http://www.mtv.com/thinkmtv/about/pdfs/APMTV_happinesspoll.pdf

Califano, Jr., J. A. 2009. *How to Raise a Drug-Free Kid.* New York: Fireside.

Carskadon, M. A. 2002. *Adolescent Sleep Patterns: Biological, Social, and Psychological Influences.* New York: Cambridge University Press.

Cohen-Sandler, R. 2006. *Stressed-Out Girls: Helping Them Survive in the Age of Pressure.* New York: Penguin Books.

Doe, M. 2004. *Nurturing Your Teenager's Soul.* New York: Perigee.

Emmons, R. A., and McCullough, M. E. 2003. "Counting Blessings versus Burdens: An Experimental Investigation of Gratitude and Subjective Well-Being in Daily Life." *Journal of Personality and Social Psychology* 84: 377–89.

Gilbert, D. 2006. *Stumbling on Happiness*. New York: Alfred A. Knopf.

Lamontagne, S. 2010. "Daily Media Use Among Children and Teens Up Dramatically from Five Years Ago." Kaiser Family Foundation. Accessed April 12, 2010. www .kff.org/entmedia/entmedia012010nr.cfm.

Lyubomirsky, S. 2007. *The How of Happiness*. New York: Penguin Books.

National Institute on Drug Abuse. 2010. *NIDA InfoFacts: High School and Youth Trends*. Accessed September 20, 2010. www.drugabuse.gov/infofacts/hsyouthtrends.html.

Pope, D. 2008. "SOS: Stressed Out Students." Lecture presented at the Challenge Success Fall Conference, Stanford University, Palo Alto, CA. challengesuccess.org.

Seligman, M. 2002. *Authentic Happiness*. New York: Free Press.

Siegel, D. 2007. *Mindful Brain*. New York: W. W. Norton.

Simmons, R. 2002. *Odd Girl Out*. New York: Harcourt.

Steinberg, L. D., and W. Steinberg. 1994. *Crossing Paths: How Your Child's Adolescence Triggers Your Own Crisis*. New York: Simon & Schuster.

Strauch, B. 2004. *The Primal Teen*. New York: Anchor Books.

University of Minnesota. 2002. "Later Start Times for Students." Accessed February 3, 2011. www.cehd.umn.edu/research/highlights/Sleep/default.html.

YMCA Parent and Teen Final Report. 2000. *"Talking with Teens."* Accessed April 3, 2009. http://clinton4.nara.gov/WH/EOP/First_Lady/html/teens/survey.html.

Lucie Hemmen, PhD, is a licensed clinical psychologist who has worked for over twenty years to strengthen communication between teens and parents. The mother of two teen daughters named Marley and Daisy, Hemmen lives and practices in Santa Cruz, CA.

MORE BOOKS *from*
NEW HARBINGER PUBLICATIONS

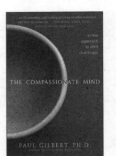

THE COMPASSIONATE MIND

A New Approach to
Life's Challenges

US $24.95 / ISBN 978-1572248403

*Also available as an e-book
at newharbinger.com*

THE COMPASSIONATE-MIND GUIDE TO BUILDING SOCIAL CONFIDENCE

Using Compassion-Focused
Therapy to Overcome Shyness
& Social Anxiety

US $16.95 / ISBN 978-1572249769

*Also available as an e-book
at newharbinger.com*

SELF-ESTEEM, THIRD EDITION

US $17.95 / ISBN 978-1572241985

*Also available as an e-book
at newharbinger.com*

WHEN PERFECT ISN'T GOOD ENOUGH, SECOND EDITION

Strategies for Coping
with Perfectionism

US $18.95 / ISBN 978-1572245594

*Also available as an e-book
at newharbinger.com*

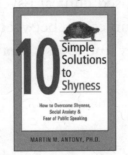

10 SIMPLE SOLUTIONS TO SHYNESS

How to Overcome Shyness,
Social Anxiety & Fear
of Public Speaking

US $16.95 / ISBN 978-1572243484

*Also available as an e-book
at newharbinger.com*

THE WORRIER'S GUIDE TO OVERCOMING PROCRASTINATION

Breaking Free from Anxiety
That Holds You Back

US $19.95 / ISBN 978-1572248717

*Also available as an e-book
at newharbinger.com*

newharbingerpublications, inc.
1-800-748-6273 / newharbinger.com

Like us on Facebook

Follow us on Twitter
@newharbinger.com

(VISA, MC, AMEX / prices subject to change without notice)

Don't miss out on new books in the subjects that interest you.
Sign up for our **Book Alerts** at **newharbinger.com**

Check out www.psychsolve.com

Psych*Solve*® offers help with diagnosis, including treatment information on mental health
issues, such as depression, bipolar disorder, anxiety, phobias, stress and trauma,
relationship problems, eating disorders, chronic pain, and many other disorders.